MASTERS OF PHOTOGRAPHY

MASTERS OF PHOTOGRAPHY

EDITED AND WITH AN INTRODUCTION BY

BEAUMONT AND NANCY NEWHALL

PARK LANE, NEW YORK

This edition is published by Park Lane,
distributed by Crown Publishers, Inc.,
by arrangement with George Braziller, Inc.
h g f e d c b
PARK LANE 1981 EDITION

Manufactured in the United States of America

Library of Congress Cataloging in Publication Data

Main entry under title:

Masters of photography.

    Originally published: New York : Braziller, 1958.
    Bibliography: p.
    Includes index.
    1. Photography, Artistic.   2. Photographers.
I. Newhall, Beaumont, 1908-   . II. Newhall,
Nancy Wynne.   III. Title.
TR650.M39   1981   799'.092'2   81-11100
ISBN 0-517-34805-5   AACR2

CONTENTS

INTRODUCTION

For more than a century, certain extraordinary men and women have worked in photography with the unmistakable authority of genius. Each of them has produced unforgettable images, and not once or twice, but again and again, and often throughout the change and evolution of a lifetime. Each is like an eye which, once opened on the universe, cannot be closed again. It is through such eyes, looking not only outward but inward, that we here present photography as a medium.

In the main body of this book, some seventeen of these masters are presented together. Each stands by himself, in the full scope and character of his work, so far as the brief compass of one crowded volume allows; each, in his life history, if he has expressed himself in words, speaks to us of what he did and why and how his own approach, his way of working, and his philosophy toward photography developed.

In this introduction, we present a synthesis of what they have known and felt about their medium. One after another, they tell us of the curious, intense and vital experience of working in photography, of its challenges, of the stages of growth it demands, the sudden revelations it presents. From their testimony there emerges a concept of photography as a medium that is very different from the casual and rather stereotyped impressions most of us have held till now.

"The camera became my companion," said Edward Weston of the first one he was given as a boy in 1902. "I lived for the hours when I could be alone with it."[1] * And thirty years later he wrote of what his 8x10 inch camera meant to him:

> My eyes are no more than scouts . . . the camera's eye may entirely change my original idea, even switch me to different subject matter. So I start out with my mind as free from image as the silver film on which I am to record, and I hope as sensitive. Then, indeed, putting one's head under the focusing cloth is a thrill, just as exciting to me today as when I was a boy. To pivot the camera slowly around watching the image change on the ground glass is a revelation, one becomes a discoverer. seeing a new world through the lens. And finally the complete idea is there, and completely revealed. *One must feel definitely, fully, before the exposure.*[2]

Man and camera become a unit, leaping ahead of conscious intention. Henri Cartier-Bresson calls his miniature camera "the extension of my eye." Through its viewfinder he discovers the world:

> In photography there is a new kind of plasticity, product of the instantaneous lines made by the movement of the subject. . . . But inside movement there is one moment at which the elements in motion are in balance. Photography must seize upon this moment and hold immobile the equilibrium of it. . . . Sometimes it happens that you stall, delay, wait for something to happen. Sometimes you have the feeling that here are all the makings of a picture—except for just one thing that seems to be missing. But what one thing? Perhaps someone suddenly walks into your range of view. You follow his progress through the viewfinder. You wait and wait, and then finally you press the button—and you depart with the feeling (though you don't know why) that you've really got something. Later . . . you'll observe that, if the shutter was released at the

* Superior figures refer to "Sources of Quotations," page 190.

decisive moment, you have instinctively fixed a geometric pattern without which the photograph would have been both formless and lifeless. . . . Composition must be one of our constant preoccupations, but at the moment of shooting it can stem only from our intuition. . . .[3]

And Weston, when his friend the painter Jean Charlot proposed to "work out the geometric plan from some of your photographs, which are so exact as to appear calculated," replied, "No, Jean, to stop and calculate would be to miss most of them."[4]

Again and again photographers insist that the instant—at once perception, composition, creation—explodes out of any confining "rules" or "laws" of composition. Julia Margaret Cameron, explaining her remarkable use of focus: "When focusing and coming to something on the ground glass which, to my eye, was extremely beautiful, I stopped there."[5] Weston summed up what the masters of photography all really feel: "Composition is the strongest way of seeing."[1]

In the instant when the exposure is made there is a further challenge: the photographer is transfixed by time. Cartier-Bresson advises:

. . . You cannot be sure in advance exactly how the situation, the scene, is going to unfold. You must stay with the scene, just in case the elements of the situation shoot off from the core again. . . . Of all the means of expression, photography is the only one that fixes forever the precise and transitory instant. We photographers deal in things which are continually vanishing, and when they have vanished, there is no contrivance on earth which can make them come back again. We cannot develop and print a memory.[3]

In a deeper sense, the instant is crucial, for photography is an instrument for truth, and it reveals who is behind the camera even more mercilessly than who or what is in front of it. Paul Strand puts it:

. . . the camera machine cannot evade the objects which are in front of it. No more can the photographer. He can choose these objects, arrange and exclude, before exposure, but not afterwards. . . . Your photography is a record of your living, for any one who really sees.[6]

Cartier-Bresson:

I believe that, through the act of living, the discovery of oneself is made concurrently with the discovery of the world around us. . . . A balance must be established between these two worlds—the one inside us and the one outside us. As the result of a constant reciprocal process, both these worlds come to form a single one.[3]

And this is the eternal challenge that holds the photographer: the two realities within and without, both limitless, for which he and his camera are a bridge.

Such a goal cannot be attained by merely factual recording. As Edward Weston wrote:

How little subject matter counts in the ultimate reaction! If there is any symbolism in my work, it can only be in a very broad consideration of life, the seeing of parts, fragments, as universal symbols, the understanding of relativity everywhere. All basic forms are so closely related as to be visually equivalent. . . . I have had a back (before close inspection) taken for a pear, knees for shell forms, a squash for a flower, and rocks for almost everything imaginable![7]

Most major photographers have at one time or other been challenged on subject matter. Weston, accused of being "theatrical" in his photographs of the natural forms of the West, replied: "Everything in the West is on a grander scale, more intense, more vital, dramatic. . . . All these forms are my neighbors, my friends. I do not lie about them. . . . If with clear vision I have seen more than the average person sees,—well, that's my job."[7]

When the power of Alfred Stieglitz's portraits was attributed to the extraordinary personalities of his sitters and his own "hypnotic effect" upon them, he chose entirely new subject matter—clouds.

I wanted to photograph clouds to find out what I had learned in 40 years about photography. Through clouds to put down my philosophy of life—to show that my photographs were not due to subject matter—not to special trees, or faces, or interiors, to special privileges—clouds were there for everyone—no tax as yet on them—free. So I began to work with the clouds—and it was great excitement—daily for weeks.[8]

He wrote Hart Crane:

I'm most curious to see what the 'Clouds' will do to you. About six people have seen them . . . all are affected greatly and forget photography entirely. . . .'I know exactly *what* I have photographed. I know I have done something that has never been done.'[9]

What he had done in this series which he called "Equivalents" was to crystallize what usually remains in the unconscious, felt rather than known. He proved that the photographer works with connotations as a poet does with words, that in intensifying, penetrating, transforming, expanding, compressing our visual connotations, he works with light and time as the musician does with sound and time.

In his *Equivalents*, in which visual connotations transcend subject matter, Stieglitz showed the way to a new medium which we are just beginning to explore: the juxtaposition of words and pictures in a way that goes beyond the conventional descriptive caption. Words evoke connotations and so do photographs; a phrase can suddenly illumine a photograph with a meaning hitherto unsuspected. In its current form of the photo essay, words launch a line of thought into the image or series of images and then carry the impulse developing forward. Good writing can rescue poor photographs, and good layout assist both, but where the image is really powerful it speaks first. Something of this power undoubtedly goes back to the fact that both as a race and as individuals we saw long before we could speak, and we have still to be taught to read and write. Words are symbols of experience; a photograph convinces us it is experience itself.

Many photographers feel closer to music than to any other medium. When they try to describe the inner how and why of photography, they resort to musical terminology. Ansel Adams, a concert pianist until he was 28, compares the experience of viewing a fine print "to the experience of a symphony—appreciation of the broad, melodic line, while important, is by no means all. The wealth of detail, forms, values—the minute but vital significances revealed so exquisitely by the lens—deserves exploration and appreciation. It takes time to *really* see a fine print. . . ."[10]

Weston:

When I can feel a Bach fugue in my work, I know I have arrived.[11]

And Stieglitz, planning his first series of *Equivalents,* clouds and hilltops, which he called "Songs of the Sky":

> I knew exactly what I was after . . . a series of photographs [over] which Ernest Bloch . . . would exclaim, Music! Music! Man, why that is music! How did you ever do that? And he would point to violins, and flutes, and oboes, and brass, full of enthusiasm. . . . And when finally I had my series of ten photographs printed, and Bloch saw them—what I said I wanted to happen, happened *verbatim.*[8]

By now it must be apparent that photography and painting widely diverge from their common base. The painter begins with pigment, itself a sensuous delight, and whether he is making an abstraction or painting the roof of the Sistine Chapel, adds to that delight with every touch and twist of the brush under his hand.

The photographer faces the challenge of severe limitations: light acting in a flash on a chemistry of silver a micron or two deep. He does not have the painter's opportunity to reconsider, transpose, eliminate, augment. He must, in an instant, create enduring beauty out of transient actuality. To Edward Steichen, long experienced both in painting and photography,

> There are only two problems in photography. One is how to conquer light. The other is how to capture a moment of reality just as you release the shutter. . . . Every man must learn to work out those two problems for himself.[12]

Many photographers have painted and many painters have photographed. To a few, the mediums are for a few years like right and left hands. But one or the other eventually dominates. Attempts to mix photography and painting fail. And at heart your true photographer resents any attempt to force photography to produce results which superficially resemble paintings. On this point the masters are unanimous: the photographic image must not be tampered with. For them, the work of any human hand is clumsy, any piecing together of negatives glaringly false, any cropping not envisaged before exposure an admission of weakness. In the darkroom these photographers use controls, but only those which enhance conviction, which help convey the truth behind the illusion. This conviction, this truth, is destroyed if negative or print is retouched.

Edward Weston came to the conclusion that photography is the most pure and direct means of expression man has yet found: conception and realization occur almost simultaneously, and the artist, undeterred by the slow and clumsy hand, is limited only by his own capacity to create.

To most major photographers there is, as Stieglitz put it, no art, there are only artists, and the uncanny perceptions which photographers possess for great artists in other mediums bear this out. Stieglitz and Steichen, for instance, introduced to America and sometimes to the world such then unknown revolutionaries as Picasso, Matisse, Cézanne, Renoir, Brancusi. And the same recognition has been accorded to photographers by painters, as witness Rivera, Siqueiros and Orozco hailing Edward Weston as one of the few authentic masters of 20th century art, and Picasso exclaiming over Stieglitz's *Steerage,* which his colleagues had dismissed as a split image, "This man is working in the same direction I am!"[13]

To non-photographers—that is, people whose main interests are elsewhere, whether or not they click an occasional shutter—and to neophytes, the first surprise in photography is how *un*mechanical it is. It is not an automatic eye. It will not see what you want it to see until you have mastered it. And by that time the chances are that what you thought you wanted to see seems distressingly dull and obvious; you have just discovered a new and subtle beauty, purely photographic, which challenges every resource of mind, heart, eye, spirit and body you possess.

The next surprise—but that is too weak a word—is that photography's apparent ease is its most frightening delusion, and one which lures millions into an abyss they do not know how to climb out of. Let us suppose that your control of your camera is now close to reflex action, that you have acquired all the basic skills, that you are plagued no more than the masters by the still primitive complexities of paraphernalia or by what Ansel Adams calls "the perversity of the inanimate." Where are you? Probably making essays in the style of some master whose vision is stronger than your own. You must learn to see for yourself and the process is as long and arduous as in any other medium. This often fills the impatient neophyte with dismay. But there is no short cut.

The third surprise is the astonishing scope this so-called "machine medium" gives to those who master it. Look at the three who begin this book: Hill and Adamson in Edinburgh, Southworth and Hawes in Boston, and Nadar in Paris. They are all primarily portraitists dedicated to the task of recording the leading figures of their time and place. Contrast the kindly nobility, the sunlit shimmer of Hill and Adamson with the deep and brilliant "power comprehending power"[14] of Southworth and Hawes whose majestic portraits, as a critic once remarked, make "beauty in a man seem trivial."[14] Then Nadar, impaling with his lens against a plain background, under a diffuse north light, the magnificence and beauty of his friends. Then consider Julia Margaret Cameron, in the idyllic and pre-Raphaelite England of the 1860s, using blur like a full brush to round out of chiaroscuro the ardent splendor, the living, breathing impact of poets and fair women. Compare within the work of one man an evolution in approach: Steichen as a young man in the 1900s seeing Wagnerian visions of the great and, in his maturity, in the 1920s and 1930s, seeing in them, as equals, their charm, their beauty, their individual genius.

Compare the interpreters of place: the resounding clarity of O'Sullivan making believable the Far West of America when it was unknown territory, the misty sparkle and lyric freshness of Emerson in East Anglia, the strange humor and wry love of Atget and the mirroring, echoing forms of past and present in his Paris of the early 20th century; Walker Evans with his nostalgic affection for the folk dreams America built into its architecture. Compare the eye witnesses of history:* Gardner and O'Sullivan calling the world to witness the impact of war on men in their photographs of Civil War battlefields; Dorothea Lange, whose sense of pathos and tragedy, of individuals caught by forces beyond their control, is Greek in its intensity, calling Americans

* Mathew B. Brady is omitted because evidence quite clearly points to him as a pictorial historian, collector and publisher, rather than as a photographer. As early as 1851 the professional *Photographic and Fine Art Journal* noted that he was "not an operator himself, a failing eyesight precluding the possibility of his using the camera with any certainty, but he is an excellent artist nevertheless—understands his business so perfectly, and gathers around him the first talent to be found." And again, in 1854, in the same magazine: "Although Mr. Brady is not a practical operator, yet he displays superior management in his business." He had already shown his historical interests in 1850, with the publication of a series of lithographic portraits, *The Gallery of Illustrious Americans*. When the Civil War broke out he organized teams of photographers. "I had men in all parts of the Army," he said, "like a rich newspaper."[15]

to witness the impact on themselves of wasting resources of land and people. And Cartier-Bresson, using the instant to lasso with a line like Daumier's, the weird, or witty, or heartbreaking appositions of reality.

Compare what, to masters in their maturity, is the personal significance of their two great tools: light and time. Weston, for whom light and time are a sculptor's chisel; Strand, who will wait years if necessary for the moment when the basic images of a land and a people, their aspirations and their destiny, are perfectly revealed, and for whom light must never be external, an accident of sun or weather, but seemingly internal, as if emanating from his subject itself, so that a face glows or pales with the life behind it, wood has the incandescence of velvet or silver, a grass blade the velocity of a steel blade. Stieglitz, for whom the moment when both past and future are visible is the crucial moment; light—any light—will do, for rain, shadow or splintered sunlight, he is light's master. Adams, for whom light and time are what music must have been to Bach; he will travel hundreds of miles, he will return again and again, until at last light and time together bring forth the moment of miracle, the mood he can take like a melody and set against the stern, exquisite counterpoint, harmony, dissonance of substance, to make a psalm, a prayer, a hosanna from the profound relation between humanity and the universe.

Of all the surprises in store for young photographers and nonphotographers, the greatest is that, in their majestic maturity, the masters one and all resign their individuality. They tear it from themselves. The paradox here, of course, is that, as Lincoln Kirstein once wrote of Cartier-Bresson, ". . . the more he effaces himself, the more he becomes the crystal eye, the more his pictures sign themselves."[16] Edward Weston: "In trying to summarize my work, I would say that in my ego of several years ago, my aim was interpretation. Now it is *significant presentation of the thing itself*—without evasion in spirit or technique—with photographic beauty."[4] This attitude has in it humility, love, deep dedication. To Cartier-Bresson: "Cynicism is the worst thing because it kills everything. There's no more honesty, no more poetry, no more freshness. . . . This is death. It kills creation. There's no love, no tenderness. . . . There's no hatred even, there's nothing."[17] To Ansel Adams, "Some photographers take reality as the sculptors take wood and stone and impose upon it the dominations of their own thought and spirit. Others come before reality more tenderly, and a photograph to them is an instrument of love and revelation."[18] And Stieglitz summed up for photographers what photography means as a life work:

"Photography is my passion. The search for truth my obsession."[19]

MASTERS OF PHOTOGRAPHY

DAVID OCTAVIUS HILL and ROBERT ADAMSON

DAVID OCTAVIUS HILL, born Perth, Scotland, 1802. Painter of romantic landscapes; interested in new techniques and movements in the arts. At 19, used the then still strange technique of lithography to bring out, through his father's publishing house, a series of Scottish landscapes. At 24, helped found the Scottish Academy of Arts; in 1830, became its secretary and served until shortly before he died. His oils and watercolors of Scotland—poetic sunsets, ancient castles, craggy seashores, lochs and highlands—engraved on steel to illustrate the collected works of Robert Burns and James Hogg.

A friend of his, Sir David Brewster, physicist concerned with optics, was deeply interested in the new technique of photography, and particularly in the paper process called the calotype; Hill appears to have tried his hand at making a few calotypes in the early 1840s.

Then in May, 1843, he witnessed an historic event: 470 clerics withdrew from the Presbyterian Church and founded the Free Church of Scotland. Hill determined to paint this great moment. He was not a portrait painter; many of the clergymen would soon return to remote parishes. He thought of the calotype and asked Brewster for advice. Brewster recommended as assistant the younger brother of his colleague, the chemist Sir John Adamson,

ROBERT ADAMSON, born Burnside, Scotland, 1821, who had already been making calotype portraits for a year.

By September, 1843, Hill and Adamson are known to have been at work on the vast assembly of clergymen. Hill moved to Rock House, at the foot of Carlton Hill, whose summit looks over Edinburgh, the Firth of Forth, and the Highlands. Here he fitted out a photographic laboratory for Adamson and a studio for his second wife, Amelia Patton, portrait sculptor with commissions to execute for the Scott Memorial.

Word of this unusual project spread; distinguished men and women came to observe and stayed to be photographed themselves. Even in full sunlight, they had to hold still at least 40 seconds; they leaned against the walls of Rock House or sat in armchairs against the darkness of its open doors, with their hands propped up on books or some tool or symbol of their interests and professions. It was an adventure into the new world of science, for those in front as well as behind the camera.

More than 1000 portraits were made between 1843 and 1848. In addition, Hill and Adamson made views of Edinburgh—Greyfriars, the Scott Memorial, John Knox's House, the Castle, St. Andrews; they went to Newhaven, a fishing village whose pastor was campaigning for a new design in fishing boats that would save the lives of his parishioners, and who enlisted the convincing calotype to help reach his audience—perhaps the earliest use of photography for a documentary or journalistic purpose.

But in 1847 Adamson had to leave; he went to St. Andrews and died, aged 27, in January, 1848. Hill is reported to have made a few calotypes after he left, but he soon ceased and went back to painting landscapes. The monstrous painting of the Founders of the Free Church of Scotland was not finished until 1866, and only then because, it is said, his wife urged it as his duty. It shows no such handling of light and character as the calotypes themselves, nor do the photographs Hill made in 1857–1862 with one A. McGlashon as partner.

During Hill's long final illness, his wife built from her earnings as a sculptor the pleasant house in Newington where, in 1870, Hill died. No obituary mentioned the photographs which in the 1850s had been privately and publicly hailed as greater than Rembrandt's etchings.

From 1870 to 1872, Thomas Annan, a friend of Hill's, who had photographed the Free Church painting for reproduction, lived in Rock House. There his son, J. Craig Annan, himself a distinguished photographer, became fascinated by the Hill and Adamson portraits. He collected the widely scattered paper negatives, made new prints and fine photogravures from them, and sent examples to Whistler and other leading painters for comment. Excited rediscovery; in 1898, Hill and Adamson were shown by the Royal Photographic Society at the Crystal Palace, London; in 1899 they were exhibited in Hamburg; in 1905 they were shown at "291," New York, and Annan's gravures published in *Camera Work* by Stieglitz. In 1931, Heinrich Schwarz brought out *David Octavius Hill, Master of Photography*, Leipzig and New York, 1931; London, 1932; the first scholarly monograph on a photographer.

John Henning. sculptor. Calotype, 1848 or earlier. George Eastman House, Rochester, N. Y.   15

16   Miss Chalmers and brother. Calotype. 1848 or earlier. Collection R. O. Dougan. Perth, Scotland.

Lady Mary Ruthven. Calotype, 1848 or earlier. George Eastman House, Rochester, N. Y.   17

18   Mrs. Rigby and her daughter, Lady Elizabeth Eastlake. Calotype, before 1848. George Eastman House, Rochester, N. Y.

George Meikle Kemp, architect of the Sir Walter Scott Monument, Edinburgh. From a calotype negative, 1844 or earlier, in the George Eastman House, Rochester, N. Y.

20   At the Greyfriars' Cemetery in Edinburgh; D. O. Hill standing at left. Calotype, 1848 or earlier. George Eastman House, Rochester, N. Y.

Fishwife, Newhaven, Scotland. Calotype, 1848 or earlier. George Eastman House, Rochester, N. Y.

ALBERT SANDS SOUTHWORTH and JOSIAH JOHNSON HAWES

ALBERT SANDS SOUTHWORTH, born in West Fairlee, Vermont, 1811. Attended Phillips Academy, Andover, Mass. In spring of 1840 saw on display in Boston the first daguerreotypes brought to America by Francois Gouraud, agent of Daguerre. Immediately determined to learn how to make them. His schoolmate, Joseph Pennell, was assisting Samuel F. B. Morse, painter, inventor of the telegraph, and one of the first to open a daguerreotype gallery in New York City; Southworth visited him and bought a camera. "I cannot in a letter describe all the wonders of this Apparatus," he wrote his sister. "Suffice it to say that I can now make a *perfect* picture in one hour's time, that would take a Painter weeks to draw. The picture is represented *light and shade,* nicer by far than any Steel engraving you ever saw."[20]

Opened a daguerreotype gallery with Pennell in Cabotville (now Chicopee), Mass., 1840. "We doubt not that in a month we shall be able to take Portraits and Miniatures to perfection."[20] By September he wrote, "I have succeeded in managing the Daguerreotype so as to make perfect likenesses. . . . In a fair day it requires three minutes sitting and we know positively that we can have an apparatus that will not require more than thirty seconds."[20]

Moved to Boston, 1841. Southworth to sister: "Our prospects are at present flattering. Our miniatures are by far the best in America, probably in the world."[20] Sent 22 daguerreotypes to Third Exhibition of Massachusetts Charitable Mechanic Association, 1841; voted "the best exhibited." In the course of the year took as partner

JOSIAH JOHNSON HAWES, who was born in East Sudbury (now Wayland), Mass., 1808. He had been apprenticed to a carpenter, and while practicing his trade as a journeyman became entranced with painting. "I practiced painting on ivory, likewise portraits in oil, landscapes, etc., with no teacher but my books," he recollected.[21] On seeing Gouraud's daguerreotypes in Boston, 1840, "gave up painting and commenced daguerreotypy. As I was one of the first in the business, I had the whole field before me."[21] A business card imprinted "Hawes & Somerby" indicates that he had a partner before joining Southworth in 1841.

The firm was known as "A. S. Southworth & Co." until Joseph Pennell retired in 1845, when the style was changed to "Southworth & Hawes." Hawes married Southworth's sister Nancy, who specialized in coloring daguerreotypes, 1847. During the 1840s and '50s the firm not only operated a gallery, but ran an extensive business in daguerreotype supplies: cameras by Voigtländer, plates by Scovill, chemicals, cases by Brady, accessories. Also taught process; their students traveled far and wide in New England.

To the Southworth & Hawes gallery at 5½ Tremont Row came American leaders: statesmen, writers, actors. The partners boasted that they never employed an "operator" (i.e. cameraman), but posed each sitter personally. "The superiority of our Likenesses is the result of our care in the arrangement throughout, particularly of the Light," they wrote in a broadside.[22] They avoided standard poses, and seized the character of the sitter with a spontaneity unusual for the day. "What is to be done is obliged to be done quickly," Southworth wrote. "The whole character of the sitter is to be read at first sight; the whole likeness, as it shall appear when finished, is to be seen at first, in each and all its details, and in their unity and combinations. . . . It is required and should be the aim of the artist-photographer to produce in the likeness the best possible character and finest expression of which that particular face or figure could ever have been capable. But in the result there is to be no departure from truth in the delineation and representation of beauty, and expression, and character."[23]

Unlike most daguerreotypists, took several exposures at each sitting; the best specimens were taken by the customer. As a result quantities of duplicate plates have survived.

Took landscapes, city views, interiors, as well as portraits, often pushing the medium beyond its accepted limits: the clipper ship *Champion of the Seas* "under all sail by the wind;" the operating room of the Massachusetts General Hospital; a schoolroom full of girls. Specialized in taking informal portraits of children.

Pioneered in America in three-dimensional photography. Built in 1853 the "Grand Parlor Stereoscope," for viewing twelve pairs of whole-plate (6½ x 8½ inch) daguerreotypes.

Southworth went around Cape Horn to the California gold fields in 1849. His quest unsuccessful. "There is little dependence to be put upon the future in any particular,"[1] he wrote his wife in 1850, who replied: "Mr. Hawes . . . wants to know whether if you had a Daguerreotype Apparatus there through the rainy season you would not make it more profitable at the mines?"[1] On returning to Boston, perfected a plate holder "to bring in rapid succession different parts of the same plate . . . into the center of the field of the lens,"[24] which he patented in 1855. His right to this patent bitterly contested by photographers the country over who had long used similar devices; patent rendered invalid by court decision, 1876. Died Charlestown, Mass., 1894.

Hawes continued studio at same location. Although he reluctantly gave up the daguerreotype process about 1861 for glass negatives and tintypes, he preserved thousands of daguerreotypes not taken by customers. These mostly now at Metropolitan Museum of Art, New York, and George Eastman House, Rochester, N. Y. Died at Crawford's Notch, N. H., 1901.

Chief Justice Lemuel Shaw of the Massachusetts Supreme Court. Daguerreotype, 1851. The Metropolitan Museum of Art, New York (Gift of I. N. P. Stokes & the Hawes family, 1937).

24   Mrs. James R. Vincent, Boston actress. Daguerreotype, about 1855. Society for the Preservation of New England Antiquities, Boston.

Sleeping baby. Daguerreotype, about 1850. Collection Ansel Adams, San Francisco.   25

(TOP) Henry Clay. Daguerreotype, about 1850. The Metropolitan Museum of Art, New York

(BOTTOM) Harriet Beecher Stowe, author of *Uncle Tom's Cabin*. Daguerreotype, about 1850. The Metropolitan Museum of Art, New York (Gift of I. N.
P. Stokes & the Hawes family).

The Boston Athenaeum. Daguerreotype, 1853. George Eastman House, Rochester, N. Y.   27

28   John Quincy Adams. Daguerreotype, about 1848. The Metropolitan Museum of Art, New York (Gift of I. N. P. Stokes & the Hawes family, 1937).

Daniel Webster. Daguerreotype, 1850. The Metropolitan Museum of Art, New York (Gift of I. N. P. Stokes & the Hawes family).   29

Cunard steamship *Niagara* in drydock, Boston. Daguerreotype, about 1850. Collection Richard Parker, Marblehead, Mass.

NADAR

Born in Paris, 1820: real name Gaspard-Félix Tournachon. Youth spent in Lyons, where his father had a publishing house, and Paris, where he received elementary education. Returned to Lyons to study medicine, which he disliked. In 1838 his father's publishing business failed. To make a living, wrote articles for Lyons newspapers signed "Nadar." Settled in Paris, 1842. Taught himself to draw, perhaps with encouragement of distant relative Gavarni, and contributed caricatures as well as literary pieces to periodicals.

In Paris lived the extravagant Latin Quarter life described by his friend Henri Murger in his novel, *La Vie de Bohème*. Founded the "Club of Water Drinkers," where art and literature were discussed. Became friend of leading artists and writers. During 1848 Revolution attempted to join revolutionists in Poland, but was interned in Germany for the duration of the uprisings.

Founded *La Revue Comique*, 1849. Upon marrying, began to look for a more satisfactory way of making a living than free-lance writing when a friend told him of a photographic outfit for sale. At first shocked by this suggestion, which seemed a betrayal of his artist friends, he learned the collodion process and in 1853 opened a photographic studio, soon to become a favorite meeting place for such celebrities as the artists Eugène Delacroix, Gustave Doré, writers Théophile Gautier, Charles Baudelaire, composers Giacomo Rossini and Giacomo Meyerbeer. Nadar photographed these friends and other famous Parisians with directness, simplicity, and dignity. Used his photographs as models for his "Panthéon-Nadar," an oversize lithograph (32 x 42 inches) containing 270 caricatures, announced in 1854 but not published until 1857.

Conceived and patented idea of taking photographs from balloon for purpose of mapmaking and surveying, 1855. Claimed to have taken aerial photographs in 1856, but earliest existing examples were made in 1858. Became passionately interested in flying and built the world's largest gas balloon, *Le Géant*, capable of carrying 49 men in its two-story car. First ascension, from the Champ de Mars, Paris, 1863. On third ascension, in same year, anchors failed to hold while descending near Hanover, Germany; Nadar and his companions were dragged for several hours across fields. Nadar broke both legs; his wife badly injured. Gave up ballooning, except for short periods during the Siege of Paris in the Franco-Prussian war of 1870, when he was in charge of Balloon Corps.

A ceaseless experimenter, began to use electric light in his studio in 1858 and two years later made a series of artificial light photographs of the sewers and catacombs of Paris.

About 1886 his son Paul took charge of Paris studio. Opened business in manufacture and sale of photographic apparatus; became the Paris dealer for George Eastman. Conceived basic plan for pioneer picture story: "photo interview" with Michel-Eugène Chevreul consisting of 21 photographs of the 100-year-old scientist, each caption with the words he spoke at time exposure was made; published in four pages of *Le Journal Illustré*, 1886. Founded magazine *Paris-Photographe*, 1891.

Throughout his career wrote extensively: autobiographical essays (*Mémoires du Géant*, 1864; *L'Hotellerie des Coquecigrues*, 1880; *Quand j'étais étudiant*, 1881; *Sous l'incendie*, 1882; *Le Monde où on patague*, 1883, *Quand j'étais photographe*, about 1900), satirical essays, novels. Was better known for his writing than for photography when he died in Paris, 1910.

The Nadar collection, numbering several thousand negatives of celebrities in the artistic, literary and theatrical world, is now preserved in the Bibliothèque Nationale, Paris.

Gustave Doré. About 1855. From the collodion negative in the Bibliothèque Nationale, Paris. 33

(TOP) Honoré Daumier. About 1855. George Eastman House, Rochester, N. Y.

34   (BOTTOM) Théophile Gautier. About 1855. Collection Georges Sirot, Paris.

Eugène Delacroix. 1855. From the collodion negative in the Bibliothèque Nationale, Paris.   35

36   Sarah Bernhardt. 1859. From the collodion negative in the Bibliothèque Nationale, Paris.

Charles Baudelaire. 1855. From the collodion negative in the Bibliothèque Nationale, Paris.   37

ALEXANDER GARDNER

Born in Paisley, Scotland, 1821. Trained in physics and chemistry; became accomplished photographer. Believing in Robert Owen's labor reforms—trade unions, education, socialist communities—came to United States in 1849 to found ideal community on the Mississippi in Iowa. Returned to Glasgow to lecture, write, and enlist other settlers. Brought own family, 1856; on landing in Newfoundland, learned many of Iowa community were stricken by "galloping consumption." Rushed to look after orphaned niece and to help survivors, but took own family to New York City. There hired by Mathew B. Brady.

Opened gallery in Washington for Brady, 1858; ran it so efficiently that profits helped support more lavish New York gallery. At the outbreak of hostilities between North and South, war views became so popular, and were so frequently pirated, that copyrighting them became essential. Brady maintained that the work of any photographer in his employ was his to copyright in his name; Gardner insisted that what a photographer did on his own time with his own equipment belonged to him; he should copyright and profit from the sale. On this they split; Gardner resigned.

Joined headquarters staff of General George McClellan as Official Photographer to the Army of the Potomac; attached to U. S. Topographical Engineers, made copies of maps and documents. As "the only artist who had free access to the Army and its Headquarters at all times as well in active movements as in camp,"[25] he and the best of the photographers who had worked under him at Brady's— O'Sullivan, Barnard, Woodbury, Foux, Gibson, his own brother James, among others—traveled with the army in their darkroom wagons; the glass plates had to be flowed, sensitized, exposed and developed within ten minutes. Personally took some of the most famous Civil War photographs: Lincoln at Antietam, the last portrait of Lincoln; the hanging of the Lincoln conspirators.

In 1863 opened own gallery in Washington. Published War Views in competition with Brady, giving meticulous credit to each photographer. Supplied photographs to *Harper's Weekly, Leslie's Illustrated News*—and also to Brady. At war's end, published two magnificent folio volumes, each containing fifty original 8 x 10 inch prints, *The Photographic Sketchbook of the War.* When, in 1869, Brady petitioned Congress to purchase his collection of war views, Gardner presented a similar petition four days later, in which he claimed "that at the outbreak of the Rebellion he conceived the idea of furnishing of it, a consecutive Photographic History." As evidence, submitted the two volumes of the *Sketchbook* "which form a small portion of the collection. Without wishing to disparage the labors of others, he believes and is so advised that there is no such collection extant. . . ."[25] Both petitions shelved. Eventually the government acquired the collections, which are now in the National Archives and the Library of Congress.

Financed trip of photographer friend Henry Moulton to Peru; made albums from these negatives: *Rays of Sunlight from South America.*

1867: to Kansas as official photographer for Union Pacific Railroad, Eastern Division; made stereographs of prairies, wagon trains, log cabins, peace treaty with Indians. 1867-1880: photographed Indian delegates to Congress for Office of Indian Affairs. Made rogues' gallery for Washington police, 1873. Gradually lost interest in photography; devoted himself to philanthropy. Died, Washington, 1882.

TIMOTHY H. O'SULLIVAN

Born in New York City, probably around 1840. Learned photography at Brady's New York gallery; then worked as cameraman under Alexander Gardner in Brady's Washington gallery. During Civil War, served six months as First Lieutenant on Gen. E. L. Viele's staff; after honorable discharge, 1862, worked for Gardner as superintendent of map work and on the battlefronts. Is reported to have photographed calmly through bombardments, had his camera twice knocked down by shell fragments. Of the 100 photographs in Gardner's *Photographic Sketchbook of the War,* 45 are by O'Sullivan.

In 1867, '68, '69, photographed for the Surveys along the 40th Parallel, led by the brilliant young Clarence King through the scarcely explored mountains and deserts of the West. Saved a boat and men in it by plunging into the rapids of the Truckee River and swimming with a rope to shore. In Nevada, descended into the mines of the great Comstock Lode; made probably the earliest mine photographs underground with magnesium powder ignited in an open tray. His darkroom usually an old army ambulance. Often commanded side explorations on his own, to photograph the Survey's findings in their clearest forms and most revealing lights.

Joined Commander Thomas O. Selfridge on the first of his surveys to seek a practical ship canal across the Isthmus of Darien, now Panama. John Moran, brother of Thomas Moran the painter, is listed as official photographer for the Darien Surveys in 1871. Yet the photographs of the enchanting Pacific Coast the Survey reached that year are credited to O'Sullivan, who may well have been there en route to join Wheeler on the first expedition *up* the Colorado River. Wheeler gave O'Sullivan a boat, promptly christened "The Picture," a crew, and instructions to photograph independently, reporting to main expedition on specified dates. The river, whose rapids overturned boats and swallowed supplies and instruments until the whole party faced starvation. Nevertheless O'Sullivan made nearly 300 negatives. Wheeler declared, "A more unique series have hardly been produced on this continent."[26] Nearly all the negatives, including those of the Grand Canyon itself, were ruined during the long journey back down the Colorado, around to San Francisco and thence to Washington.

In 1873, O'Sullivan joined Wheeler again, during his explorations of Arizona and New Mexico, photographing the desert, its strange ecology, and multiple layers of civilization—the then mysterious cliff dwellings, the Indians, nomad and pueblo, the Spanish towns. 1880: Clarence King, now director of U. S. Geological Survey, gave him temporary employment. Appointed chief photographer to the Treasury, November, 1880; removed, March, 1881. Died of tuberculosis at the house of a relative in Staten Island, January, 1882.

O'Sullivan: Gen. U. S. Grant and staff officers. Massapomax Church, Virginia. May 21, 1864. From the collodion negative in the Library of Congress, Washington, D. C.

Gardner: President Abraham Lincoln on the battlefield of Antietam. 1862. George Eastman House, Rochester, N. Y.

40   Gardner: Home of a rebel sharpshooter. Gettysburg. Pa. 1863. George Eastman House, Rochester, N. Y.

O'Sullivan: A Harvest of Death. Gettysburg. Pa. 1863. George Eastman House, Rochester, N. Y.

42   Gardner: Ruins of arsenal, Richmond, Virginia. 1863. George Eastman House, Rochester, N. Y.

O'Sullivan: Quarters of men in Fort Sedgwick, generally known as Fort Hell. 1865. George Eastman House. Rochester. N. Y.

(TOP) O'Sullivan: Start of Government expedition up the Colorado River, from Camp Mojave, Arizona. 1871.

44   (BOTTOM) O'Sullivan: Black Cañon, Colorado River. 1871. Authors' collection.

O'Sullivan: Ancient Ruins in the Cañon de Chelle, New Mexico. 1873. Authors' collection.

JULIA MARGARET CAMERON

Born in Calcutta, 1815; third and only homely daughter of James Pattle, high official in Bengal Civil Service, known as "the biggest liar in India."[27] Her six sisters, beauties, yet double all their other gifts—wit, generosity, a high hand—ascribed to her. Educated in France and England. Married Charles Hay Cameron, also high official in British Civil Service, 1838. In absence of viceroy's wife, became leader of Anglo-Indian society. Became friend and correspondent of many of the most famous people of her time.

To England, 1848; became intimate of Watts, Rossetti and others of the Pre-Raphaelite movement. In 1859 moved to Freshwater, Isle of Wight, to be near Tennyson. Given camera and equipment for processing collodian plates in 1864 by daughter and son-in-law: "It may amuse you, mother, to photograph. . . ."[5] Turned chicken coop into a studio, coal bin into a darkroom. "From the first moment," she wrote in her *Annals of My Glass House*, "I handled my lens with a tender ardour. . . . I longed to arrest all beauty that came before me. . . ."[5] Ruined quantities of table linen with silver nitrate stains by rushing to show her husband each "fresh glory. . . . I should have been banished from any less indulgent household."[5] Her technique deplored by professional photographers. Grandchildren were posed with swans' wings and crowns of flowers, parlormaids draped as the Madonna. "Even more than photography," wrote an undoubted eyewitness, "female beauty was Mrs. Cameron's passion. Her household staff was a dream of fair women. . . . She herself was charmingly, hopelessly, pathetically plain and knew it."[28] Dominated friends into sitting for hours in rugs and berets. Tennyson, her most frequent

victim but helpless to resist her, remarked on leaving Longfellow, "You'll have to do whatever she tells you. I'll come back soon and see what is left of you."[29] Carlyle, who had feared his sitting as "a kind of inferno," wrote her of the results: "It is as if suddenly the portrait began to speak, terrifically ugly and woebegone. . . ."[29] Of his portraits and those of Sir John Herschel she wrote; "When I have had such men before my camera, my whole soul has endeavoured to do its duty towards them in recording faithfully the greatness of the inner man as well as the features of the outer man. The photograph thus taken has been almost the embodiment of a prayer."[5] 1866–70: finest portraits of great men and beautiful women; of the *Mountain Nymph*, Herschel wrote: "She is absolutely alive and thrusting out her head from the paper into the air. This is your own special style."[5] 1870–75: illustrations to poetry, including Tennyson's *Idylls of the King:* period described by Gernsheim as "amateur theatricals."[29] Not even unknown tourists were safe from capture as Guinevere, nor Mr. Cameron from posing hours in a hollow oak as Merlin. Her portraits hailed by painters, scientists and writers from her day till now.

In 1875 her husband being in poor health and longing for the East, and their income sadly depleted by her generosities, she suddenly decided they should leave for Ceylon; embarked with a cow and two coffins, in case none were available there. Returned briefly to England, 1878. Continued to photograph in Ceylon, mostly native types. Died there, her last word being, "Beautiful!"[27] in 1879.

The Mountain Nymph, Sweet Liberty. 1867. George Eastman House, Rochester, N. Y.

48   Alfred, Lord Tennyson. 1865. George Eastman House, Rochester, N. Y.

Henry Wadsworth Longfellow. 1868. The Museum of Fine Arts. Boston.   49

50   Mrs. Herbert Duckworth (later Mrs. Leslie Stephens), mother of Virginia Woolf. 1867. George Eastman House, Rochester, N. Y.

Ellen Terry. 1864. The Metropolitan Museum of Art (Alfred Stieglitz Collection, 1949).   51

52   Thomas Carlyle. 1867. George Eastman House, Rochester, N. Y.

Sir John Herschel. 1867. The Museum of Fine Art. Boston.   53

PETER HENRY EMERSON

Born in Cuba, 1856. Father American, a doctor, first cousin to Ralph Waldo Emerson; mother English. Boyhood in Massachusetts. After father's death, mother returned to England with children. Henry educated at Cambridge; acquired degrees, including one in medicine. Settled in Southwold, Suffolk. Fascinated by the strange amphibian lives of the peasants and fisherfolk of East Anglia, began an ethnic study of them; took photographs. In 1882 joined what is now the Royal Photographic Society; shocked by photographic exhibitions crowded from floor to ceiling by "art photographs" sentimentalizing peasant life, and by huge, sharp, slick "combination prints" made to imitate fashionable genre painting by piecing together several negatives of fake settings and models in costume. Started reading about art; horrified to discover it based not on scientific first principles but the constantly shifting tastes of experts.

With a painter friend, T. F. Goodall, explored current art theory of Naturalism; approved fidelity to Nature as scientific first principle for art, and fidelity to actual human vision, according to Helmholtz's theory that the eye sees sharply only in the center, as the kind of focus essential in photography as an art. Photographed real people in real life and real landscape.

In 1885, suddenly burst into the exhibitions, winning prizes and medals with his photographs, and into the magazines with a barrage of articles. Extolled the beauty of the ground glass image as unattainable by hand or eye; urged painters to use it as scientists use microscope and telescope. Pronounced photography superior to any other graphic medium; in fact, "should photography in colours ever be perfected, let painting look to herself, for she will tremble in the balance."[30] Called for photographs to be as beautiful as watercolors or etchings, and as simply mounted and framed; called for photography to be exhibited with the dignity of art—one picture per frame, hung on the line, judged and installed by artists. Recommended two new processes: the platinotype, a paper with fine tooth and a long scale of delicate grays, and photogravure, made under the photographer's supervision, as printing mediums worthy of photography as an art.

Brought out in 1886, in collaboration with Goodall, *Life and Landscape on the Norfolk Broads*, first of his six albums presenting through poetic photographs and text by turns lyric, scientific, indignant, "truthful pictures of East Anglian Peasant and Fisherfolk Life, and of the landscape in which such life is lived."[31] Its forty platinum prints hailed as "epoch-making." Elected to Council of Royal Photographic Society to represent the new and fast-increasing legion of amateurs. Lectured before Camera Club Conference, attacking art criticism as "pernicious illogical literature" and Ruskin as "a spasmodic elegant" promoting "false stones in a setting of fine writing," denouncing H. P. Robinson, the "uncrowned king" of combination printing, as a "wiseacre" and his enormously successful handbook, *Pictorial Effect in Photography*, as "the quintessence of literary fallacies and art anachronism."[32] Sensation: by 1887 Emerson acclaimed "the leader of a new school of art photography." Made sole judge of *The Amateur Photographer's* Holiday Work Competition, awarded first prize for "truly spontaneous quality" to

a young American student then working in Germany, Alfred Stieglitz.

In 1889, Emerson's handbook, *Naturalistic Photography*, burst on the photographic scene like "a bombshell dropped in a teaparty." Skimming through art history from a Naturalistic viewpoint, dismissed medieval painting as "distorted types of repulsive asceticism," Michelangelo as "'a lover of pathological specimens," and admirers of such benighted works as "frugivorous apes." Bolstered his theory of "differential focussing" with scientific and optical facts. Stated classic esthetic, ethic, and technique of pure photography as independent art: 1. *Simplicity of means.* "Lightness [of equipment] may even be harmful, as leading to overproduction." Gadgets "are apt to become deranged and finally to embarrass the worker at a critical moment." 2. *Truth to subject.* No faking by lighting, posing, costuming, props. "The true photographer . . . must have his camera ready . . . and when he sees his model in an unconscious and beautiful pose, he must snap his shutter." 3. *Free composition, without rules or formulae.* "Each picture requires a special composition, and every artist treats each picture originally. . . . The point is, *what you have to say and how to say it.*" 4. *The pure photographic image.* "Retouching is the process by which a good, bad, or indifferent photograph is converted into a bad drawing or painting. . . . Avoid retouching in all its forms; it destroys texture and tone and therefore the truth of the picture."

Violent controversy ensued between his followers and his enemies, especially over composition and focus. Then, in 1890, came a still bigger bombshell: In a black-bordered pamphlet, *The Death of Naturalistic Photography* he states that (1) "conversations with a great artist" caused him to doubt nature as a scientific first principle for art: "To you then, who ask an explanation of my conduct, art—as Whistler said—*is not* nature . . .;" and, (2) that the experiments of Hurter and Driffield, which established the mathematical relation between exposure, density and development, caused him to doubt photography's potentials as an art: "the all-vital powers of selection and rejection are *fatally* limited. . . ." He withdrew all remaining copies of *Naturalistic Photography*.

But even he could not stop what he had started. The idea of photography as an art in its own right, first as individual expression and later as the discipline of "pure" photography went on inspiring photographers to found movements and societies, issue manifestoes, work through changing and evolving concepts. And Emerson himself, though his bitter new opinion remained unchanged, went on serving on juries, writing articles, publishing albums, and even an expurged and expanded third edition of *Naturalistic Photography*, 1899. The Royal Photographic Society in 1895 awarded him its high honor, the Progress Medal for his work in the advancement of artistic photography, and in 1900 held a retrospective exhibition of his photographs. In 1925 he began awarding medals for "artistic merit" to photographers living or dead, known or unknown: the list includes Hill and Adamson, Bayard, Cameron, Nadar, Craig Annan, Brassï. Worked on a history of artistic photography; reported it "just finished," 1933. Died, 1936.

Gathering Waterlilies. Platinum print, 1886. George Eastman House, Rochester, N. Y.   55

P.H.EMERSO

A Slippery Path—Winter Scene, Norfolk. Photogravure in *East Anglian Life*, 1888. George Eastman House, Rochester, N. Y.

Gunner Working Up to Fowl. Platinum print, 1886. The Museum of Modern Art, New York.   57

Dyke Scene, Norfolk Broads. Platinum print, 1886.

Norfolk Cottages. Photogravure in *East Anglian Life*, 1888. George Eastman House, Rochester, N. Y.

Waiting for the Tide, Cantley. Platinum print. 1886. George Eastman House, Rochester, N. Y.

ALFRED STIEGLITZ

Born of German immigrants in Hoboken, New Jersey, on January 1, 1864. Father achieved a fortune modest but sufficient for six children; retired; built brownstone in upper Manhattan and summer home at Lake George; formed Sunday salon, mostly of artists, where the word business was forbidden. In 1881 took family to Europe for five years.

Alfred entered Berlin Polytechnic to study mechanical engineering, but, after buying a camera and starting to photograph in sheer exuberance, switched to study photography under Hermann Vogel, discoverer of dye-sensitization of photographic emulsions and champion of pictorial photography according to H. P. Robinson. Rigorous training: Alfred, already at 19 a perfectionist, stuck to assignments until Vogel explained that the absolute is unattainable. Continued, nevertheless, to push frontiers of medium, both technical and esthetic. Earliest work related to that of genre painter friends and admired by them. Agreeing with P. H. Emerson's revolutionary ideas on photography as an art, made in Italy in 1887 the first photographs he later considered significant; sent them to contest of which Emerson was sole judge; received first prize.

Was starting an "amateur" (or "creative and disinterested") movement in Germany when, in 1890, after the death of a sister, his mother begged him to come home. Lonely, uprooted, shocked to see his idealized New York in the raw misery of depression; shocked, in first and last business experience, to discover profit and exploitation replacing quality and craftsmanship as motives for both labor and management. Entered photoengraving firm, 1890; resigned, 1895; thenceforth lived on small income. Found American amateur photography flourishing but vapid. Would have fled back to Europe if a friend had not challenged him to try one of the new hand cameras, then advertised as "detective" and despised as "button-pressing" by serious photographers. Plunged into the streets and began the series on New York which he continued for forty years. Worked in storms, at night, on people in action—conditions then considered impossible. Advised by fellow camera club members to throw out his thin negatives, he made spectacular lantern slides and photogravures from them.

In 1893 took on editorship of somnolent *American Amateur Photographer*. Scandalized publisher by sending out rejection slips reading, "Technically perfect; pictorially rotten!" Magazine boomed, but Stieglitz and publisher could not see eye to eye. In 1896, when publisher reprinted a photograph without credit, Stieglitz resigned. Merged two desultory local clubs into the Camera Club of New York. Made its exhibitions and journal, *Camera Notes*, into white-hot center of photography in America. Discovered brilliant unknowns: Edward Steichen in Wisconsin, Clarence White in Ohio, Alvin Langdon Coburn in Boston. Accused of "rule-or-ruin" tactics by club members, Stieglitz withdrew in 1902 and founded the Photo-Secession and its quarterly, the great *Camera Work*. Sent exhibitions, always hung as a group, to salons everywhere; brilliant and shocking, the Photo-Secession caused international furore.

In 1905, Steichen, back from painting in Paris, suggested that rooms next to his own at 291 Fifth Avenue might serve as galleries. In the Little Galleries of the Photo-Secession, soon known as "291," Stieglitz demonstrated through exhibitions the potential of photography as an art; showed Europeans as well as Americans: pioneers Hill and Cameron as well as Steichen and other members. In 1907 came to conclusion that many photographs shown were not art but imitations of art. Personally returned to pure photography. To shock and feed photography, began showing other forms of art. Steichen, back in France, responded by sending drawings by his friend the sculptor Rodin. Soon Stieglitz was showing to an incredulous New York, for the first time in America, and sometimes anywhere, such unknown Europeans as Picasso, Matisse, Cézanne, Braque, Renoir, Rousseau, Brancusi; such unknown Americans as Marin, Hartley, Weber, Dove. Published, for the first time, in *Camera Work*, Gertrude Stein. Loved satire; in magazine "291," 1915–16, worked with Marcel Duchamp, Francis Picabia, Marius de Zayas on first Dada-Surrealist manifestation. Recognized, in the photographs of Paul Strand, "the new photography;" in watercolors sent him from Texas by a schoolteacher named Georgia O'Keeffe, "finally, a woman on paper." But, with deep roots in Germany, he could not accept the hysterias of World War I; old and staunch friends fell away. In 1917 he closed "291" and brought to an end the fifty numbers of *Camera Work*.

Alone, he poured into his own photography the phenomenal energy he had expended for the last twenty years in projects and people. Made portraits whose searching candor had dimensions in time as well as space. O'Keeffe came to New York; he made hundreds of photographs of her—the portrait of a relationship. Exhibited in 1921, these photographs, carrying the conviction that pure photography was now a mature medium of great power, hit younger photographers just recovering from the dislocation of war even harder than they hit the public. Some critics attributed their force to Stieglitz's hypnotic control over his unusual sitters; for answer, Stieglitz turned his camera up to the skies, and, at first, with the idea of making equivalents to music, photographed sun and clouds; later, sometimes adding equally common and available subjects such as dew, grass, houses, trees, with the idea of making equivalents of complex human emotions and experiences.

Meanwhile, in response to the needs of those around him, chiefly Marin, O'Keeffe, Strand, Demuth, Dove, Lachaise, Hartley, he was making exhibitions for various galleries. In 1925, opened The Intimate Gallery; in 1929 An American Place—a high corner in an office building where the light was good.

Continued exhibitions; only new artists the photographers Ansel Adams and Eliot Porter. Got prices other gallery-owners envied; when asked "How much?" asked, in turn, "How much are you ready to give the artist?" Ceased photographing; old and frail, came daily to the Place, talking to all comers, attacking prejudices, affirming integrity, art, spirit. The Place became a kind of shrine. He was alone there when, in 1946, he suffered the heart attack of which, a few days later, he died.

The Steerage. Photogravure, 1907. George Eastman House, Rochester, N. Y. 61

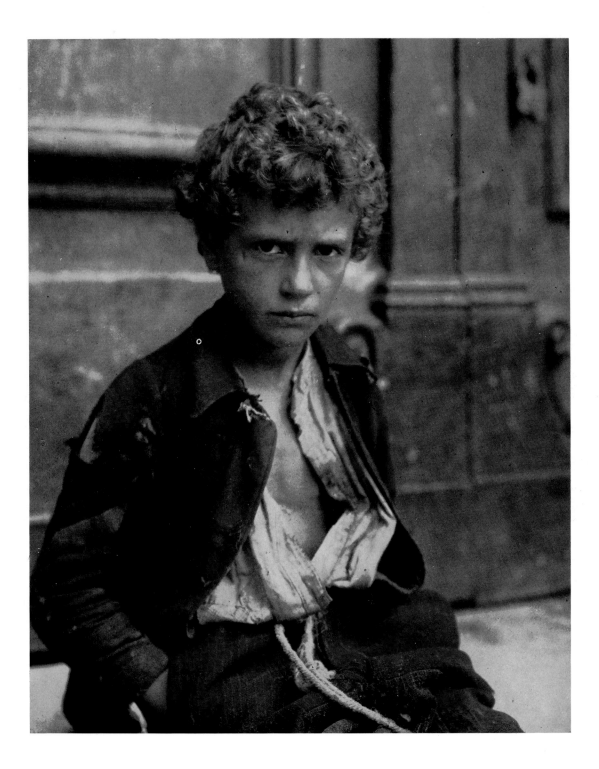

Venetian Boy. 1887. George Eastman House, Rochester, N. Y. (Alfred Stieglitz Collection).

The Terminal. Photogravure. 1893. The Museum of Modern Art. New York. 63

64   The Ferry Boat. Photogravure, 1910. George Eastman House, Rochester, N. Y.

The City of Ambition. Photogravure, 1910. George Eastman House, Rochester, N. Y.   65

66   Charles Demuth. Platinum print, 1922. The Metropolitan Museum of Art, New York (Gift of Alfred Stieglitz, 1928).

Evening from the Shelton. 1931. Collection Dorothy Norman, New York.   67

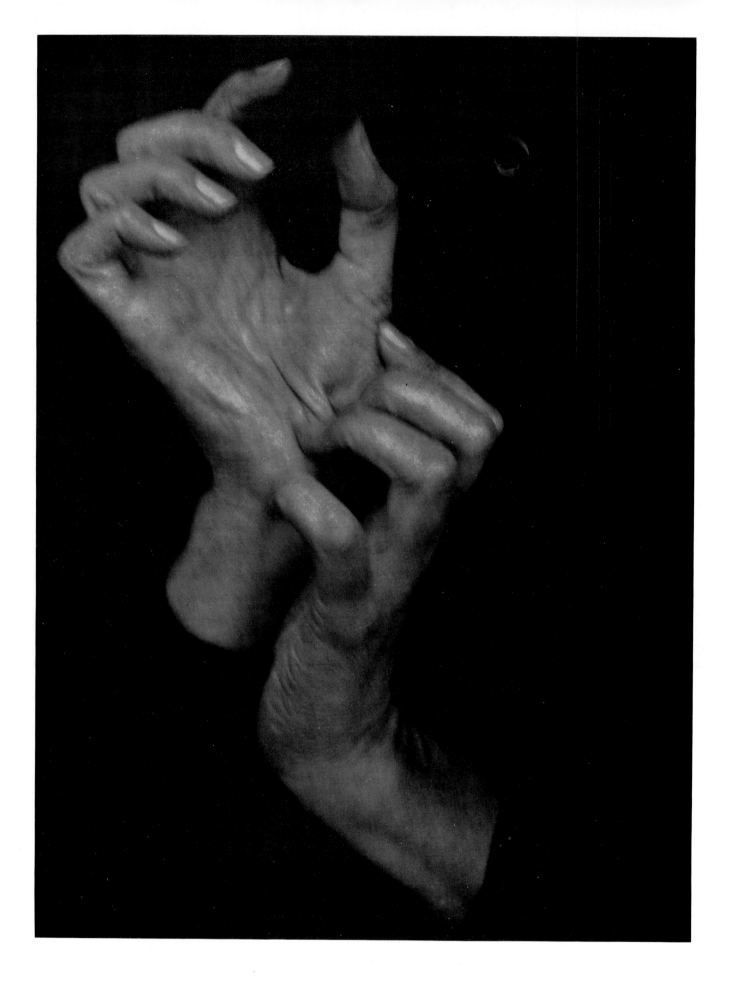

68   Georgia O'Keeffe's Hands. Palladium print, 1918. George Eastman House, Rochester, N. Y. (Alfred Stieglitz Collection).

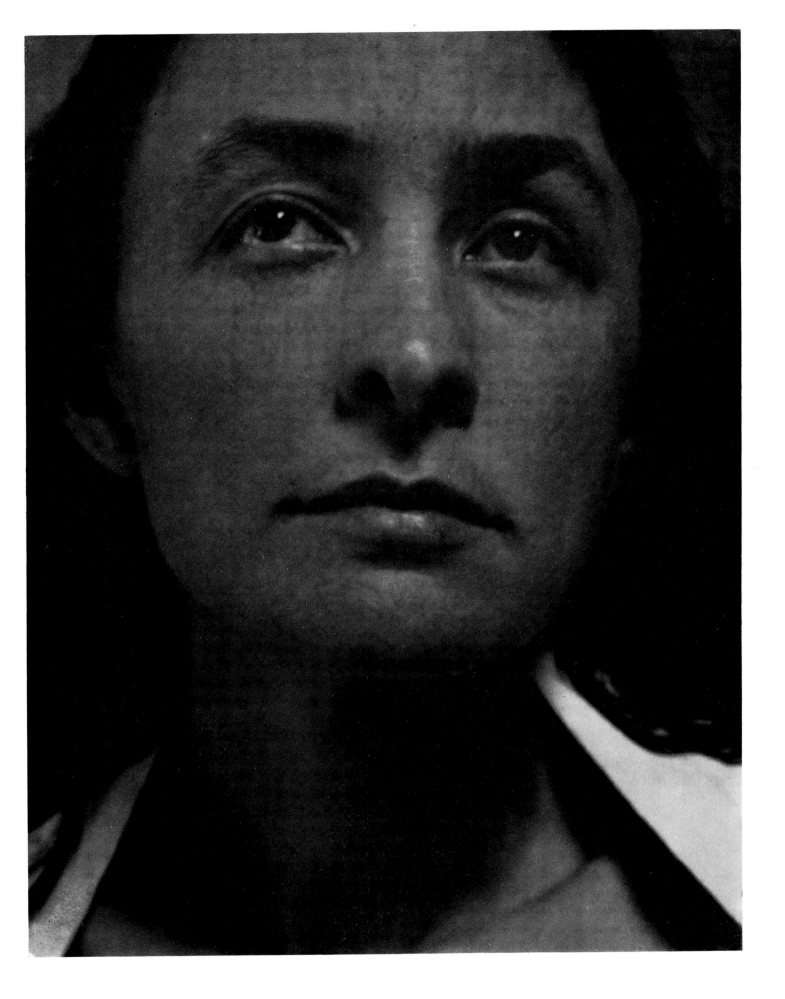

Georgia O'Keeffe. Platinum print, 1919. The Metropolitan Museum of Art, New York (The Alfred Stieglitz Collection, 1949).   69

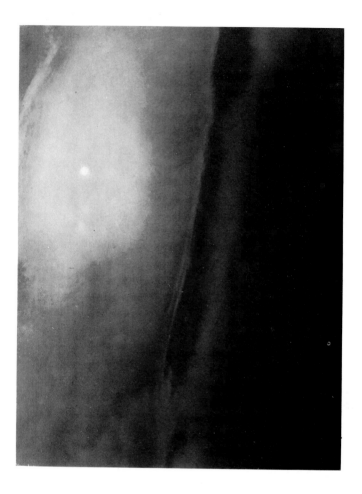

70   Equivalent. About 1931. George Eastman House, Rochester, N. Y. (Alfred Stieglitz Collection).

Georgia O'Keeffe. Palladium print, 1922. George Eastman House, Rochester, N. Y. (Alfred Stieglitz Collection).

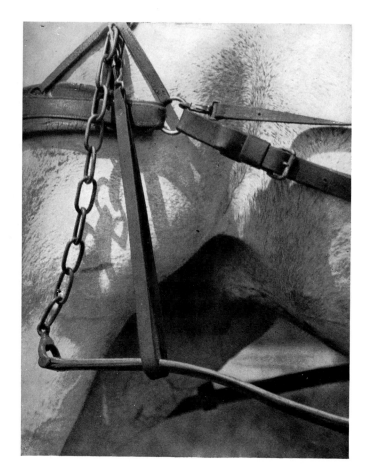

Spiritual America. 1923. George Eastman House, Rochester, N. Y. (Alfred Stieglitz Collection).

Apples and Gable, Lake George. 1922. George Eastman House, Rochester, N. Y. (Alfred Stieglitz Collection).   73

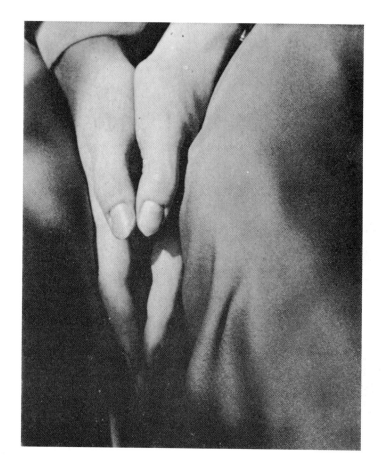

74   Hands—Dorothy Norman. 1932. Collection Dorothy Norman, New York.

Equivalent. About 1934. The Metropolitan Museum of Art, New York (The Alfred Stieglitz Collection).   75

EDWARD STEICHEN

Born Luxembourg, 1879; christened Eduard. Parents came to U. S. in 1881; settled in Hancock, Michigan. Father worked in mines, mother made hats. Sent to school in Milwaukee at 9; first attempts at drawing excited such praise from his teacher that his mother decided he must become an artist; family moved to Milwaukee. Left school at 15; was apprenticed to lithography company; continued in spare time to paint and to photograph portraits, picnic groups, etc. Organized and was first president of Milwaukee Art Students' League, setting up a school, holding exhibitions. Lithography company promoted him to designing posters. His paintings refused by Chicago Art Institute; his photographs accepted, in 1898, by Philadelphia Photographic Salon; one juror, Clarence White, wrote him in praise. In 1899, White and Stieglitz, as judges of a photography show at the Chicago Art Institute, hung most of his entries. In 1900, F. Holland Day included Steichen in his exhibition in London, *The New School of American Photography*.

In 1900, Steichen went to New York, where Stieglitz bought at $5 each the first photographs he had ever sold; then to Paris and London. Paintings accepted Paris Salon, 1901. One-man show of paintings and photographs, Paris, 1902; next year, submitted photographs labelled "drawings . . . to get them past the doorman,"[34] and accompanied by explanatory note to the jury, who accepted them. This caused such a furore that the jury, alarmed lest photographers deluge the salon in future, withdrew them.

On his return to New York in 1902, Steichen was hailed by Stieglitz as "the greatest photographer." *Camera Work* No. 2 devoted to his work. Founded with Stieglitz the Little Galleries of the Photo-Secession ("291") and designed the décor. In 1907 he and Stieglitz were among the first to experiment with the new Lumière color process, Autochrome. Stieglitz helped Steichen obtain then unheard-of fees for reproductions.

Went back to France in 1906; found work being done in a new art movement; sent to Stieglitz for exhibiting at "291" drawings by Rodin, watercolors by Cézanne and the young American John Marin; paintings and sculpture by Picasso and Matisse; sculpture by Brancusi; stage designs by Gordon Craig. Rented a small farm at Voulangis, near Paris; concentrated on painting and plant genetics. 1911: first fashion photographs for *Art et Décoration*. 1914: at outbreak of World War I returned with family to New York. In 1917, he and Stieglitz, judging a show together, created a sensation when they threw out all academic "pictorialists" and showed only "straight" photography, such as Strand and Weston.

On America's entry in World War I, Steichen was commissioned First Lieutenant in the U. S. Army; assigned to Air Service as technical advisor on aerial photography; his knowledge of people and sources in Europe proved invaluable in getting supplies. The need for absolute sharpness in reconnaissance photographs engrossed him. During 2nd Battle of the Marne was placed in command of all aerial photographic activities—55 officers, 1000 men, 5 photo squadrons. Raised to Colonel, 1918; Distinguished Service Citation from Pershing; Chevalier of Legion of Honor from France, 1919.

Returned to Voulangis. When his gardener brought him a copy of one of his paintings, Steichen felt that the copy was stronger and simpler than original, that "as a painter I was producing a high grade wall paper with a gold frame around it. . . . We pulled all the paintings I had made out into the yard and we made a bonfire of the whole thing. . . . It was a confirmation of my faith in photography, and the opening of a whole new world to me."[1] Locked himself up with his camera, and better to understand techniques and processes, began a series of experiments, during one of which he photographed a white cup and saucer on a white ground more than 1000 times. "The knowledge I had gained then became something in my bloodstream. I didn't have to stop and think. I knew just what I could expect from the sensitive material and the lenses."[34]

Returned to New York; in 1923 was hired as chief photographer for the Condé Nast publications, *Vogue* and *Vanity Fair*. Made fashion photographs human as well as elegant; in portraits of leading personalities—Chaplin, Gershwin, Mencken, Garbo, Swanson—made use of the witty or symbolic accessory. Also produced advertising illustrations. Raised standards and prices of commercial photography to new level.

In late 1930s found himself spending more time in management than photography. "The work was no longer alive. . . . It was turning out the same thing to the point where it became merchandise. . . . I just couldn't handle the thing any more so I closed up shop [January 1, 1938] and I retired."[34]

One-man show of photographs, Baltimore Museum of Art, 1938. At Ridgefield, Conn., went on with plant breeding and experiments in color photography. When America entered World War II, felt that ". . . If we could really photograph war as it was . . . in all its monstrous actuality, that could be a great deterrent for war."[34] Refused by Army Air Force because over age; accepted by Navy. Commissioned Lieutenant Commander, organized aviation photographic unit of 7 young men; stressed "the importance of photographing the men . . . the ships and planes, they would be obsolete before long, but men never get obsolete. . . ."[34]

1942: directed large and spectacular theme show, *The Road to Victory*, with text by brother-in-law, Carl Sandburg; in 1944, *Power in the Pacific*, both for the Museum of Modern Art, New York. 1944: Placed in command of all Navy combat photography; 4000 men. Supervised film, *The Fighting Lady*, in the Pacific on *U.S.S. Lexington*. Received rank of Captain; Distinguished Service Medal, 1945.

1947: became director, photography department, Museum of Modern Art. Fine Arts Medal, American Institute of Architects, 1950. At the museum, concentrated on group and theme shows, such as *The Exact Instant*. Felt a "rebirth in photography . . . instead of making pretty pictures, or technically perfect pictures, going out to get life . . . I felt that photography itself was producing a positive approach. . . ."[1] Spent three years, traveling at home and abroad, organizing great exhibition *The Family of Man*, which opened at Museum of Modern Art, January, 1955. Hailed as the greatest photographic show ever made, it brought tears and accolades, was intelligible to Paris intellectuals and illiterate tribesmen alike when it was circulated by the U. S. Information Agency throughout the world. The book made from it became a best-seller. Awarded honorary doctor's degree, University of Wisconsin, 1957.

The Blue Sky (Mrs. Steichen). Palladium print, 1923.   77

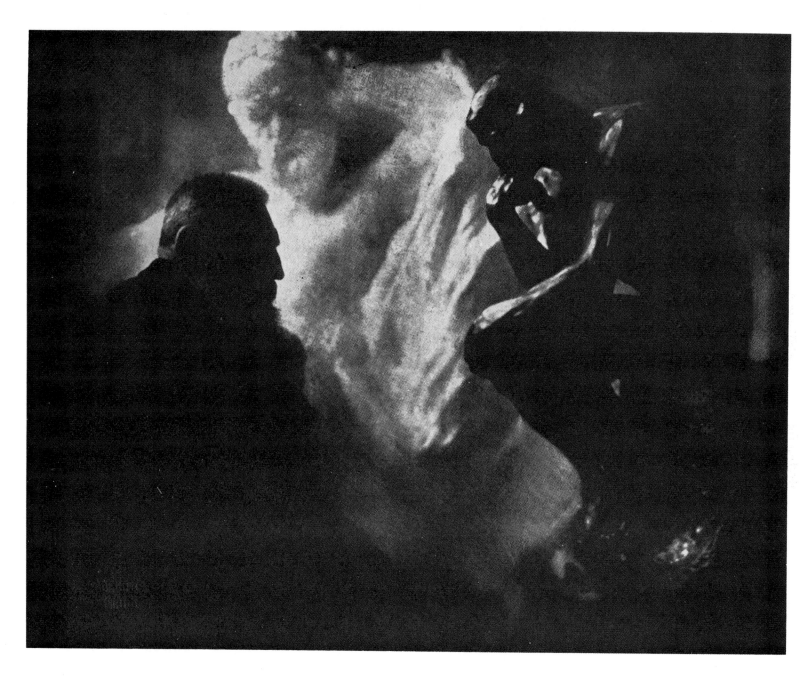

78   Rodin—Le Penseur. Gum print. 1902. Collection Hammarskiold, Stockholm.

J. Pierpont Morgan. Platinum print, 1903. The Metropolitan Museum of Art, New York (Alfred Stieglitz Collection).   79

The Flatiron Building. Platinum and ferroprussiate print. 1905. The Metropolitan Museum of Art, New York (Alfred Stieglitz Collection, 1949).

Rodin's Balzac by Moonlight, Meudon. Pigment print, 1909. The Metropolitan Museum of Art, New York (Alfred Stieglitz Collection, 1949).   81

82   President Theodore Roosevelt. Pigment print. 1908. The Museum of Modern Art. New York.

Alfred Stieglitz. Platinum print, 1909 or 1910. The Museum of Modern Art, New York.   83

84   The Empire State Building. 1932. The Museum of Modern Art, New York.

Homeless Women—The Depression. 1932. George Eastman House, Rochester, N. Y.   85

86   Isadora Duncan—Portal of the Parthenon. 1921. George Eastman House, Rochester, N. Y.

Lotus. 1922.

Gloria Swanson. 1926. For *Vanity Fair*.

Greta Garbo. 1928. For *Vanity Fair*. 89

90   Charles Chaplin. 1925. For *Vanity Fair*.

Marion Moorehouse. 1927. Fashion photograph for *Vogue*. 91

EUGÈNE ATGET

Born Jean Eugène Auguste Atget in Bordeaux, France, 1856. Parents died when he was very young; an uncle, a stationmaster, brought him up. Bordeaux being a port, going to sea was logical; the young Atget, starting as cabin boy, shipped for several voyages. Then, he turned from sailor to comedian; formed a life long attachment with an actress much older than himself. Being short and thick, Atget found himself relegated to third class roles; played the provinces and the outskirts of Paris until, when he was about 40, he realized neither he nor his companion could live by the stage any longer.

Debated what new trade to adopt; had a lively interest in painting and painters, and did some painting, rather primitive, himself. Decided finally, around 1898, according to André Calmettes, actor and pioneer motion picture director, "to be a photographer, a photographer of art; already his ambition was to create a collection of all which, in Paris or its environs, was artistic or picturesque. Immense subject."[35] Atget got a camera, and, bag on back, heavy with plates, set forth. Selling was difficult; finally he sold a print for 15 francs. "Atget encouraged was Atget saved."[35] He came to know architects, historians, editors, and painters such as Braque and Utrillo. Being shown paintings which men like Utrillo based on his photographs doubtless gave him pleasure. The playwright Victorien Sardou told him what ancient mansions, churches, shops, streets were doomed to destruction; Atget, with his old view camera, 18 x 24 centimeters, and the slow lens that didn't cover the plate when he raised the front, got there in early dawn; even so people passing left ghostly blurs on his long exposures.

Later in the day, he might ask an itinerant peddler to stand still, or set up his tripod in a room whose inhabitant had just stepped out. He was making a living; he was proud and happy. Then came World War I; he hated war; he sold little or nothing, and when peace came, he was old.

Les Monuments Historiques, however, bought from him all photographs relating to the history of Paris, especially monuments destroyed or damaged in the recent bombings. In 1921, a connoisseur named Dignimont commissioned him to document the brothels; Atget found the job annoying. Once he was arrested, and freed only after showing to the Prefecture his papers as official photographer to the City of Paris. Around 1925 a young American, the painter and photographer Man Ray, saw some of his prints at a friend's and found his eye for the strange and accidental so astonishing he published four of them in *La Révolution Surréaliste*, 1926. Sometime that year, Atget's companion died at eighty-four. Calmettes wrote: "Atget, alone, helpless, more and more bent, sad and tired, but always courageous, went on. One morning (in August, 1927) I received from Atget by messenger this tragic note traced by a desperate hand '. . . I am in agony, come quick!'—We rushed. Too late; Atget could not be saved. For twenty years he had lived on nothing but milk, bread and bits of sugar; nothing could make him admit these were not the sole useful foods and all others not the most dangerous of poisons. In art, in hygiene, he was absolute. . . . This intransigence of taste, of vision, of processes he applied to the art of photography and from it came marvels. . . . Paris will see no more that strange silhouette, that energetic face, that personage à la Balzac, always in immense threadbare overcoat and worn round hat, his hands roughened and stained by acids. He was one of the most curious men I have met . . . a strong and courageous artist, an admirable image maker."[35]

But during the last two years of Atget's life, Berenice Abbott, another young American photographer, then Man Ray's technical assistant, had been so moved by Atget's profound and poetic vision that several times she climbed the four flights to his small atelier-apartment with "Documents pour Artistes" on the door, its primitive darkroom and homemade albums. Then in the fall of 1927, she came to find everything shut and gone. Atget was dead; where were his negatives? his prints? She tracked them down, and bought them out of her own slender resources, eventually brought them to New York. For the last thirty years she has cared for these negatives, some two thousand, many of them now cracked and peeling due to the varnish Atget put on them, and thousands of the rich gold-toned prints he made on the old printing-out paper. More than anyone else, she has made what Atget saw available to the world.

Uniforms, Les Halles, Paris. About 1910. George Eastman House, Rochester, N. Y.

94   Fruit Stall, Rue Mouffetard, Paris. About 1910. George Eastman House, Rochester, N. Y.

Women, Rue Asselin, Paris. About 1920. George Eastman House, Rochester, N. Y.   95

Brothel, Versailles. About 1920. George Eastman House, Rochester, N. Y.

The Giant, Fête du Trône, Paris. About 1910. George Eastman House, Rochester, N. Y.   97

Coiffeur, Avenue de l'Observatoire, Paris. About 1920. George Eastman House, Rochester, N. Y.

Café "La Rotonde," Boulevard Montparnasse, Paris. About 1920. George Eastman House, Rochester, N. Y. 99

100   Lampshade Peddler, Paris. About 1910. George Eastman House, Rochester, N. Y.

The Eclipse, Paris, April, 1912. George Eastman House, Rochester, N. Y. 101

PAUL STRAND

Born in New York City, 1890; of Bohemian descent. Given first camera at twelve. At Ethical Culture School, studied photography under Lewis Hine, then just beginning to photograph the immigrants arriving at Ellis Island. Went with Hine and group to "291," where Stieglitz was exhibiting work of the Photo-Secession; found beauty and variety of photographs a revelation; decided, at seventeen, to become a photographer. Joined Camera Club of New York, 1908, for darkroom facilities; worked his way alone through the then current fashions in seeing and printing. Returned frequently to "291;" puzzled at first by paintings by Picasso, Cézanne, Renoir, Braque, then discovered same dynamics in El Greco and other older masters. Every year or two brought his own work to Stieglitz for comment; learned to use the same dynamics in photography and to accept its challenge to achieve art through objectivity.

"In 1915 I really became a photographer. . . ."[36] Began working with movement: New York traffic seen from above, "the hurt, eroded people" in the streets, seen close and unawares; common objects such as bowls and fences seen as forms and rhythms. Showed these to Stieglitz; immediate recognition. One-man show at "291," 1916; last two issues of *Camera Work* devoted by Stieglitz to ". . . the real Strand. The man who has actually done something from within. The photographer who has added something to what has gone before. The work is brutally direct. . . . These photographs are the direct expression of today."[37]

1918–19: X-ray technician, U. S. Army. 1921: joined unit making medical films as cameraman. With the painter and photographer Charles Sheeler, made the poetic and semi-abstract documentary film, *Manahatta*, with text from Walt Whitman. Still working closely with Stieglitz, battled for art ideals in the press, lectured on "pure" photography, wrote articles on Marin, O'Keeffe, Lachaise, helped hang exhibitions and found galleries. In personal work was photographing machines and the impact of New York City on suburb and farmland.

1922: decided to earn living as freelance motion picture cameraman through newsreels, college commencements, location footage for Hollywood. By 1926 could afford a month or two each year for personal "still" work. First summer in Colorado; realization of natural forms and forces. 1927-28, in Maine, worked close to natural forms: rocks, driftwood, a cobweb heavy with rain, a mushroom cut by grasses. Exhibited by Stieglitz at The Intimate Gallery, series described by critic Henry McBride as "the essentials of poetry."

1929: to the Gaspé; pursued moment of perfect balance—clouds, men, waves, lights—when inner meaning of a landscape is expressed. Became aware how deep was his feeling for what he later described as "the spirit of place."

1930-32: to New Mexico; deeper realization of earth and sky rhythms and of architecture as human expression. 1933, to Mexico; moved by the grace and dignity of the people, photographed them unawares in little towns and added to his interpretation the symbols of their beliefs. Appointed chief photographer and cinematographer by Mexican Government, photographed and supervised production of *Redes* (released in U. S. as *The Wave*), film about fishermen in the bay of Vera Cruz. 1935: to Moscow for six weeks; offered jobs photographing for magazine *USSR in Construction* and helping Eisenstein with new film; refused. Returned to U. S.; worked as a cameraman for U. S. documentary film, *The Plow That Broke the Plains*, directed by Pare Lorentz. 1936: second Gaspé series. 1937: Frontier Films, non-profit company to produce documentary films, formed with Strand as president.

1940: produced *Photographs of Mexico*, portfolio of fine gravure facsimiles of his rich, deep platinum paper prints.

1942: *Native Land*, on civil rights, the only film photographed for Frontier Films by Strand, released. 1943: small films for wartime government agencies.

1943-44: to Vermont in winter. Returned to still photography. 1945: one-man restrospective exhibition, Museum of Modern Art, New York. 1946–47: collaborated with Nancy Newhall in book interpreting New England through photographs integrated with a text edited from original letters, poems, essays and other writings by New Englanders; this book, *Time in New England*, published 1950.

1948: Strand to France; astonished photographers there by his magnificent prints, stately large camera equipment, unhurried approach: "I do not seek the special moment, the special expression or activity."[1] Avoided monuments; lingered in little towns and remote countrysides for a year before unlimbering his camera to make what his French collaborator, the poet and critic Claude Roy, felt were photographs so French that "I leave you to open as a family album"[38] their book, *La France de Profil*, published 1952.

Strand had long desired to make the portrait of a whole town; his Italian collaborator, the film scenarist Cesare Zavattini, suggested Luzzara, where he had been born and knew everybody. Strand found it the perfect town, basic, unpicturesque, alive. "It is one thing to photograph people; it is another to make others care about them by revealing the core of their humanness."[1] Their book, *Un Paese*, published 1954. That summer Strand started work in the Outer Hebrides with Basil Davidson, author and journalist, as collaborator, on book with working title, *Tir A' Mhurain*, (Gaelic: "Land of Bent Grass"); not yet published. Strand now living near Paris, working on series of experimental portraits. ". . . I haven't time to do more than stick to my own last, be ever more critical of what I do, and face up to the photographic and esthetic problems which life itself presents. The deeper one goes into the latter, the tougher the problems, is it not so?"[1]

Wall Street, New York, 1915. Photogravure, 1915. George Eastman House, Rochester, N. Y.   103

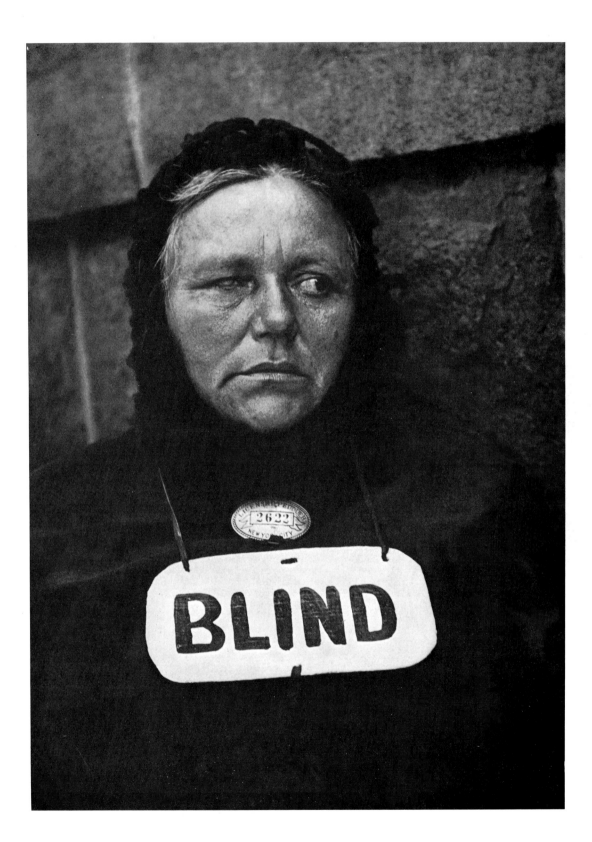

104   Blind Woman. Platinum print, 1915. The Metropolitan Museum of Art, New York (Alfred Stieglitz Collection, 1949).

The White Fence. Photogravure, 1916. George Eastman House, Rochester, New York.   105

106   The Lathe. 1923.

Fern, Early Morning. 1927   107

108   Fox River, Gaspé. 1936.

Rock, Georgetown, Maine. 1927.

(TOP) Ranchos de Taos Church. New Mexico. 1931.

110   (BOTTOM) Woman. Patzcuaro. Mexico. 1933.

Cristo with Thorns, Huexotla. Mexico. 1933.   111

112   Mr. Bennett, Vermont. 1944.

Town Hall, New England. 1946.   113

Boy, Gondeville (Charente), France, 1951. George Eastman House, Rochester, N. Y.

The Family, Luzzara, Italy. 1953.   115

Tir A' Mhurain (Land of Bent Grass), Hebrides. 1954.   117

EDWARD WESTON

Born Highland Park, Illinois, 1886, of a long line of New England preachers, teachers, and doctors. Mother's dying wish was that he escape into business. Dreamed instead of becoming a trackstar, prizefighter (bantamweight), painter. In 1902, his father gave him a Bullseye camera; thenceforth lived for the hours he could spend alone with his camera.

After three dull years as "rabbit"—errand boy and salesman—in Chicago, went on holiday to visit sister Mary in California. Stayed. Surveyed for railroads, bogus and real; then got postcard camera and punched doorbells, doing everything from babies to funerals for a dollar a dozen. Decided to become a portrait photographer and so earn a living with tools he could use for his personal work. Married Flora May Chandler, 1909; four sons born: Chandler, 1910, Brett, 1911, Neil, 1914, Cole, 1919.

In 1911 opened own studio in Tropico, now Glendale, California. Very successful, especially with babies, dancers. Trying to photograph his baby sons, he became entranced by possibilities of natural light. Began winning prizes, salon and professional, national and international, for his "high-key" portraits and unusual use of natural light—spots, shimmers, haze, dramatic shadows. Became very arty; sported a velvet cape.

Saw exhibition of modern painting, San Francisco, 1915, and began search for new dynamics, angularities, sharpness. Ceased to exhibit at salons. One day scraped the emulsions off old prize-winning negatives and used the glass in a window.

To the East, 1922; photographed steel mills in Ohio, then went to New York. Met Stieglitz, Sheeler, others, who confirmed his new direction.

To Mexico, 1923; set up portrait studio with Tina Modotti, who under his teaching became a gifted photographer. Weston welcomed by Rivera, Siqueiros, Charlot, Orozco as authentic master of 20th century art. Three years of ruthless self-scrutiny and growth; living close to a primitive people, began to search for the simple and elemental in his own work, technique, life. "Peace and an hour's time—given these, one creates," he wrote in his day-book. "Emotional heights are easily attained; peace and time are not . . . One should be able to produce significant work 365 days a year. To create should be as simple as to breathe."

In 1927, returned to California. In studio of a painter friend, found some nautilus shells, made massive closeups of them. Confined to his studio for fear of losing a chance sitter, he went on working with massive closeups of natural forms—peppers, cabbages, fruit. In flight from cities, he moved to Carmel in 1929, and discovered the amazing forms of Point Lobos—storm-twisted cypresses, wave-twisted kelp, eroded rocks. This series so excited Orozco that he arranged for and personally installed Weston's first one-man show in New York, 1930, it also led Merle Armitage to publish first book, *Art of Edward Weston*, 1932. Many shows, often accompanied by statements on pure photography and the "straight" approach. In 1931, with Ansel Adams and Willard Van Dyke, founded Group f.64, of photographers dedicated to the same ideals.

Around 1932, Weston found his camera reaching for larger themes—"My work is always a few jumps ahead of what I say about it!" Increasingly sick of portraiture,—though he hung out a sign saying UNRETOUCHED PORTRAITS and campaigned among his sitters—he longed to be free of the studio and return to landscape, which he considered the most difficult challenge a photographer can face. First landscapes mourned by fans as a decline into "hearts and flowers." Series of dunes and nudes done at Oceano, 1936.

In 1937, the first photographer to be awarded a Guggenheim Fellowship, photographed through the West; sought to test theory that whereas artists in other media are slowed by the hand into realizing only a fraction of what they conceive, a photographer, who conceives and executes almost simultaneously, in the first flash of amazement, is limited only by his own power to create. Examining the fifteen hundred eight-by-ten negatives he produced that year—the only duplicates being of moving objects—he felt their range and versatility proved the validity of "mass-production seeing." 1938: Fellowship renewed; final journeys, while son Neil built simple redwood house with darkroom in Carmel Highlands.

Married Charis Wilson, daughter of writer Harry Leon Wilson. Printed, while Charis wrote up the log of their journeys as text for *California and the West*, 1940.

1941: was photographing through the South and East for Limited Edition Club's *Leaves of Grass*, by Walt Whitman, when trip was cut short by Japanese attack on Pearl Harbor. Hurried home; served as airplane spotter on Pacific Coast. 1946: came East for opening of his one-man retrospective at the Museum of Modern Art. 1947: while Willard Van Dyke made movie of him, *An American Photographer*, for the State Department, Weston for the first time concentrated on color photography; found its potentials exciting. Already stricken with Parkinson's disease, he realized he would soon be unable to see to focus or to control his hands. Made last tremendous, tragic and intricately organized photographs at Point Lobos, 1948.

Presentation of work continued: Merle Armitage brought out *50 Photographs by Edward Weston*, 1947; Ansel Adams brought out *My Camera on Point Lobos*, 1950; major retrospectives shown in Paris and London. In 1952, with aid of son Brett, produced 50th Anniversary Portfolio of original prints. In 1955-56, the generosity of a friend enabled him to choose the thousand negatives he considered the best of his life's work; eight sets printed under his supervision by Brett. Lou Stoumen made movie *The Naked Eye*, featuring Weston's work. Died at his home in Carmel on New Year's morning, 1958, quietly.

Dunes, Oceano. 1936. George Eastman House, Rochester, N. Y.   119

120   Pulqueria, Mexico, D.F. 1926. George Eastman House, Rochester, N.Y.

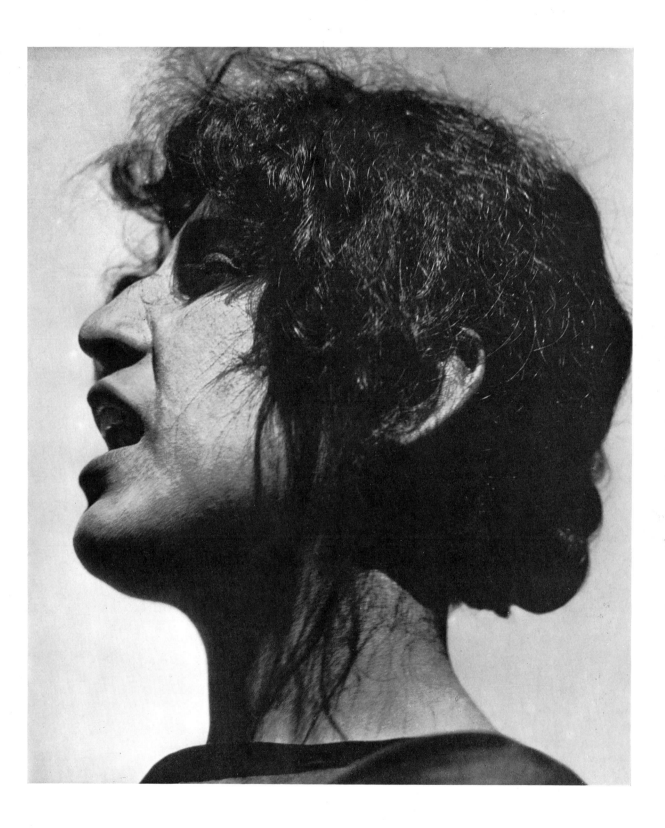

Guadalupe Marin de Rivera, Mexico. 1924. George Eastman House, Rochester, N. Y   121

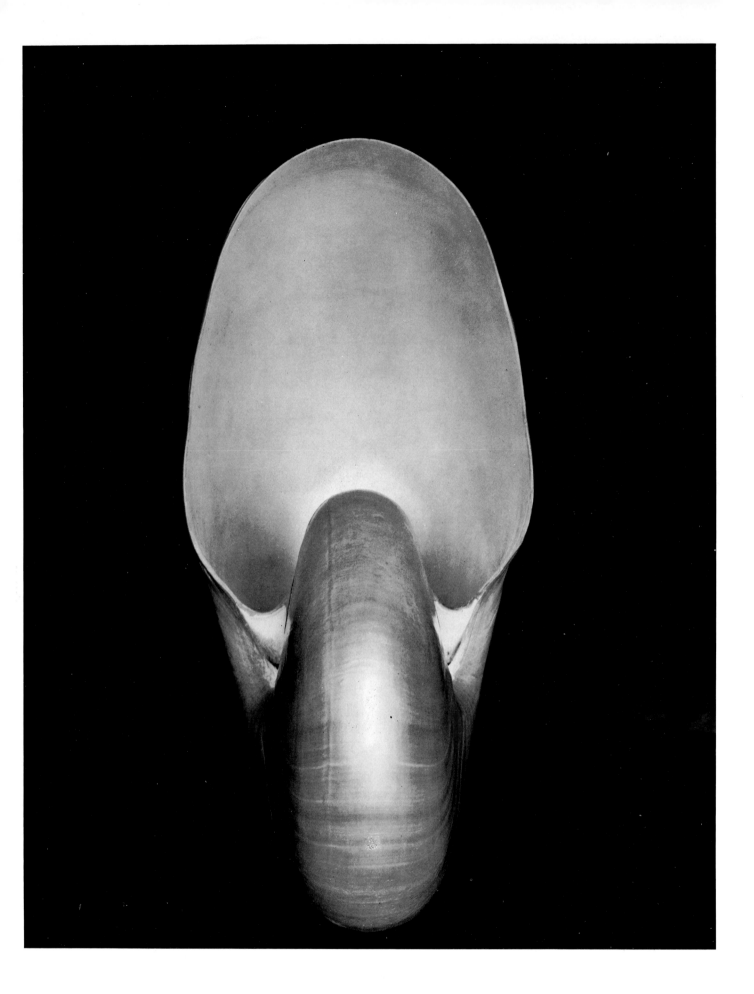

122   Shell. 1927. George Eastman House, Rochester, N. Y.

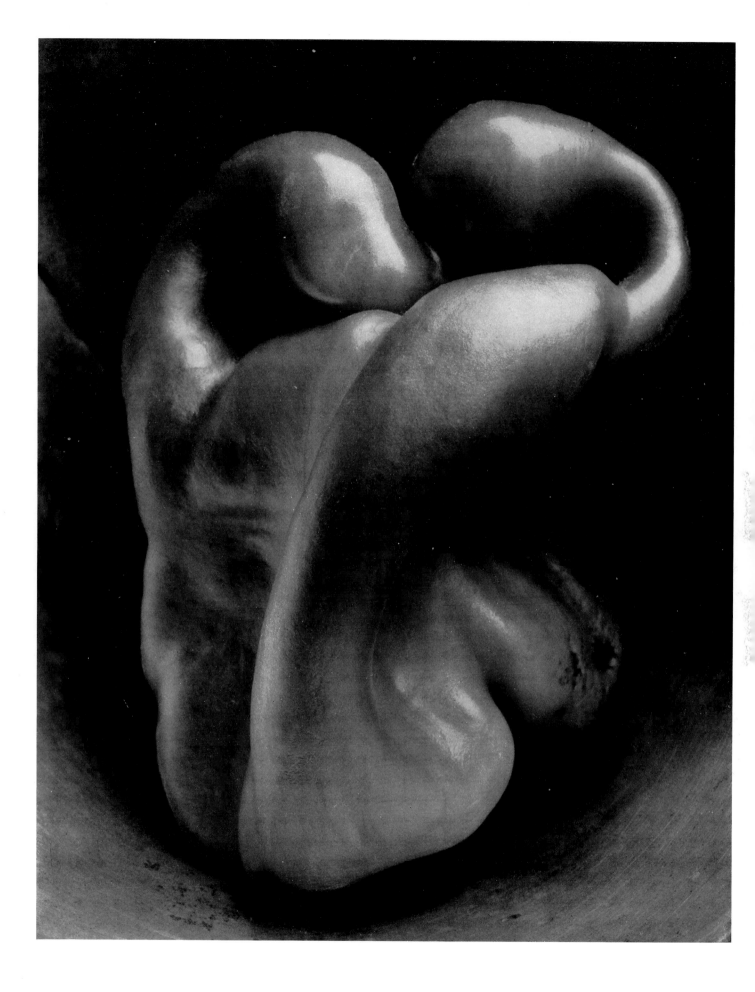

Pepper, No. 30. 1930. George Eastman House, Rochester, N. Y.   123

124   Pelican's Wing. 1931. George Eastman House, Rochester, N. Y.

Cypress Root, Point Lobos, 1929. George Eastman House, Rochester, N. Y.   125

126   Dunes, Oceano—Evening. 1936. George Eastman House. Rochester. N. Y.

Rhyolite, Nevada. 1938. George Eastman House, Rochester, N. Y.   127

128   Juniper, Sierra Nevada. 1937. George Eastman House, Rochester, N. Y.

Iceberg Lake, Sierra Nevada. 1937. George Eastman House, Rochester, N. Y.   129

130   Church Door, Hornitos, California. 1940. George Eastman House, Rochester, N. Y.

Belle Grove, Louisiana. 1941. George Eastman House, Rochester, N. Y.   131

132   Pelican, Point Lobos. 1941. George Eastman House, Rochester, N. Y.

Point Lobos. 1946. George Eastman House, Rochester, N. Y.   133

ERICH SALOMON

Born in Berlin, 1886. Early interests: zoology and carpentry. Studied mechanical engineering and law at University of Munich; gained doctor's degree. During World War I was captured by the French during the Battle of the Marne; prisoner of war for four years. In the postwar aftermath took various odd jobs, including offering legal advice to clients while driving them in the side car of his motorcycle. Finally found permanent employment in publicity department of the Ullstein Verlag, an important Berlin publishing house. Bought, in 1927, a view camera with which to record the firm's billboards. A few months later acquired one of the first miniature cameras to be fitted with an $f/2$ lens (an Ermanox, for glass plates $1\frac{5}{8}$ x $2\frac{1}{4}$ inches). This camera enabled him to take photographs indoors with relatively short exposures.

A gadgeteer—he devised for Ullstein a map which moved at the speed of a train, on which to pinpoint possible locations for billboards—he put the camera inside an attaché case and fitted levers to trip the shutter from the outside. With this disguised camera took pictures in the courtroom of a sensational murder trial, which sold so well he resigned from Ullstein's to spend all his time as a freelance.

Specialized in photographing, without supplementary lighting, inconspicuously, discreetly, meetings, conferences, social gatherings, theatrical presentations, concerts. Won the confidence of heads of state, foreign ministers, diplomats, who allowed him to set up his camera—he always used a tripod for his half-second to second exposure—in the rooms where they deliberated: the League of Nations, a palace, a capitol. French prime minister Aristide Briand

once said: "What's a meeting that isn't photographed by Salomon? People won't believe it's important at all!"[39]

His unposed portraits so striking and unusual that a British art editor called them "candid photographs." In 1929 visited England for first time. Although strictly forbidden, under penalty of punishment for committing contempt of court, to photograph the High Court of Appeal, did so. When the Lord Chief Justice saw the pictures, all was forgiven. Visited America, 1930: first European photographer allowed to work in the White House. Published, 1931, the book *Berühmte Zeitgenossen in unbewachten Augenblicken* (*Celebrated Contemporaries in Unguarded Moments*), with candid photographs of more than 170 famous people, including Briand, Pablo Casals, Albert Einstein, William Randolph Hearst, von Hindenburg, Pierre Laval, David Lloyd George, Mussolini, Thomas Mann and his brother Heinrich. "The work of a photojournalist who wants to be more than a mere craftsman," Salomon wrote, "is a constant battle, a battle for the picture, and as in hunting, he gets his game only if he has an obsession for the chase."[40]

During the Nazi regime left Germany with family for Holland. When Holland fell, went in hiding. Was betrayed by a Dutch Nazi. Last heard of on May 24, 1944—en route to the extermination camp at Auschwitz.

After the war, his negatives found in Holland—some buried in a chicken yard—by his son, Peter Hunter. First exhibition at "photokina" international photographic exposition, Cologne, 1956. First American exhibition, George Eastman House, Rochester, N. Y., 1958.

Visit of German statesmen to Rome: Mussolini. Heinrich Bruning. Dino Grandi. Julius Curtius. 1931. Collection Peter Hunter, Amsterdam.   135

(TOP) Fritjof Nansen, explorer and philanthropist with a British journalist, League of Nations, Geneva. 1928.

(BOTTOM) Max Liebermann, Berlin. 1931. Collection Peter Hunter, Amsterdam.

William Randolph Hearst at his home, San Simeon, Calif. 1930. Collection Peter Hunter, Amsterdam.

Sir Austen Chamberlain, left, talking to Gustav Stresemann, Aristide Brıand and (back to camera) Vittorio Scialoja, Lugano. 1928. Collection Pete
Hunter, Amsterdam.

The United States Supreme Court. Chief Justice Hughes presiding. 1932.

Spectators in the gallery of the League of Nations. Geneva. 1930. Collection Peter Hunter. Amsterdam.

DOROTHEA LANGE

Born Hoboken, New Jersey, 1895. Started to become a teacher but found herself becoming a photographer instead. Studied photography under Clarence White at Columbia University; worked briefly for Arnold Genthe, who gave her the first camera she ever owned. After a winter photographing children, decided, at age 20, to work her passage around the world through photography. In San Francisco, lost all her money; got a job in a camera store and liked the people she met across the counter so much she stayed. Opened a portrait studio, 1916; very successful with simple, dateless portraits. Married the painter Maynard Dixon; travelling with him in the Southwest, began to photograph outdoors, still concentrating on heads. Felt her work needed more scope; during a summer with her children in the mountains, tried to photograph nature; failed. In the middle of a thunderstorm, "it came to me that what I had to do was to take pictures and concentrate on people, only people, all kinds of people, people who paid me and people who didn't."[41]

During the early 1930s, in the depths of the Depression, watched the jobless drifting through the streets near her studio. One afternoon in 1932, with her brother as protection, took her camera down into the streets; photographed *White Angel Breadline*. Found no protection needed; found in the shocking, moving, elusive reality of the streets a new dimension: ". . . earlier, I would have thought it enough to take a picture of a man, no more. But now, I wanted to take a picture of a man as he stood in his world."[41] Thereafter worked in the streets whenever she could get free of her studio. These photographs excited Willard Van Dyke into writing about them and showing them at his studio gallery, 683 Brockhurst, Oakland. There "her eye for the essence of a situation" caught the attention of Paul Taylor, professor of economics at the University of California, who was attempting to use the camera as a research tool. In 1935, asked by the State of California to report on migrant labor, Taylor insisted on a photographer as research assistant, then an almost unprecedented request, and hired Dorothea Lange.

The jobless in the streets had mostly been silent; the landless in the tents and jalopies, torn from their farms by drought and debt, wanted to talk; she not only photographed but listened. "Their roots were all torn out. The only background they had was one of utter poverty. It's very hard to photograph a proud man against a background like that. I had to get my camera to register the things about these people that were more important than how poor they were—their pride, their strength, their spirit."[41] Taylor discovered Lange's "ear was as good as her eye," and put the bitter simple statements she heard people say beside their photographs in his report. This was so effective a presentation that the State began building camps for these refugees, and the Federal Government, in setting up the Rural Resettlement Administration (later the Farm Security Administration) included a photographic division, under Roy Stryker, to interpret their plight to the public. Dorothea Lange

and Walker Evans were among the first hired. Reproduced in thousands of newspapers and magazines, these photographs roused the conscience of the nation. Although assailed by critics as "the ashcan school" and by later politicians as "subversive," they created a style which influenced a generation of photographers and has since passed into the bloodstream of photojournalism. They inspired Archibald MacLeish to his book of "photographs illustrated by a poem," *Land of the Free*, 1938, and Sherwood Anderson to his picture book, *Home Town*, 1940; two movies also took shape from them. In 1935, Pare Lorentz, starting his film, *The Plow that Broke the Plains*, came across a Lange-Taylor report that caused him to include a sequence on the migrants in California: "I borrowed Dorothea for a week and worked with her for a day . . . One cannot say, 'That is a Dorothea Lange picture' because of any technical stylization. On the other hand, you can usually spot any of her portraits because of the terrible reality of her people. You do not find in her portrait gallery the bindle-stiffs, the drifters, the tramps, the unfortunate, aimless dregs of a country.

"Her people stand straight and look you in the eye. They have the simple dignity of people who have leaned against the wind, and worked in the sun, and owned their own land."[42] King Vidor, starting to direct John Steinbeck's *Grapes of Wrath*, got the same report from Lorentz, and used it as an index to visual authenticity.

In 1939, Lange and Taylor, who were now married, published a summation of their reports in words and pictures, *An American Exodus: A Record of Human Erosion*.

In 1941, Lange received a Guggenheim Fellowship, but resigned it after the Japanese attack on Pearl Harbor and America's entry into World War II. Photographed the hysteria-evoked evacuation of the Japanese-Americans from the Pacific Coast and their herding into concentration camps. Continued to photograph, sometimes with Ansel Adams, for several other wartime government agencies. In 1945, was warned by doctors to take it easy; asked, "How can a photographer take it easy?" Photographed the San Francisco conference establishing the United Nations; collapsed. After several years' illness, began in 1951 to photograph again.

Concentrated now on relationships: people to each other, the earth, society, the time: ". . . my own approach is based upon three considerations. First—hands off! Whatever I photograph I do not molest or tamper with or arrange. Second—a sense of place. I try to picture as part of its surroundings, as having roots. Third—a sense of time. Whatever I photograph, I try to show as having its position in the past or in the present."[41] 1954, with Ansel Adams, Taylor and her son the writer Daniel Dixon, photographed *Mormon Villages*, essay for *Life*; 1955, *The Irish Countryman*, also for *Life*; *The Public Defender*, essay on law courts; 1956-57, *The Last of a Valley*, an area evacuated and devastated as a dam site, with Pirkle Jones; 1957, *The New California*.

White Angel Breadline, San Francisco. 1932. George Eastman House, Rochester, N. Y.   141

142   Tractored Out, Childress County, Texas. 1938. George Eastman House, Rochester, N. Y.

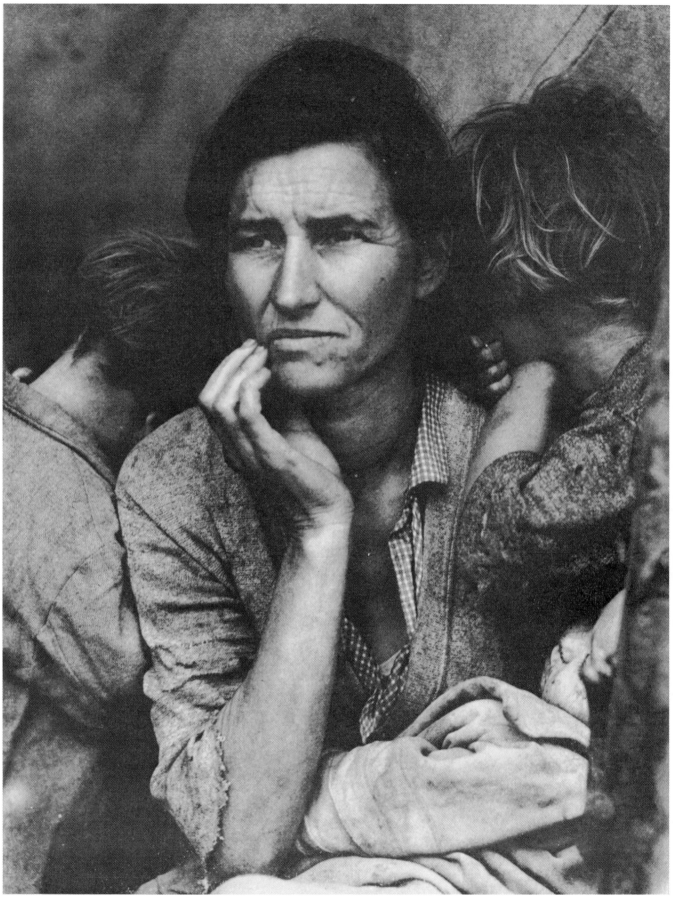

Migrant Mother, Nipomo, California. 1936. George Eastman House, Rochester, N. Y.   143

144   Delta Plantation, Mississippi. 1936.

Uprooted, San Joaquin Valley, California. 1936. George Eastman House, Rochester, N. Y.   145

146   The Defendant, Alameda County Court House, Oakland, California. 1955.

Last Ditch, Oakland, California. 1955.   147

148   Field Worker in Texas Sun Bonnet. 1936.

Freedom of Religion: Three Churches, Three Denominations, on the Great Plains. 1938.   149

WALKER EVANS

Born St. Louis, Missouri, 1903. Educated at Phillips Academy, Andover, at Williams College, and in Paris.

Began, 1930, series of photographs of Victorian and indigenous architecture, largely in New England: these exhibited at Museum of Modern Art, 1934. Illustrated special edition of Hart Crane's *The Bridge*, 1930. Exhibition at Julien Levy Gallery, New York, 1932. To Cuba, 1932: a portfolio of 28 of his photographs published in Carleton Beals' *The Crime of Cuba*, 1933. Made 500 negatives and several sets of prints of African Negro Art, for distribution by General Education Board to colleges and libraries, 1935. Joined Resettlement Administration (later Farm Security Administration) to work as photographer with Roy E. Stryker, 1935; his penetrating and revealing vision, realized precisely with view camera, was important in setting the style of this school of documentary photography. Of these photographs Lincoln Kirstein has written: "the facts of our homes and times, shown surgically, without the intrusion of the poet's or painter's comment or necessary distortion, are the unique contemporary field of the photographer. . . . It is for him to fix and to show the whole aspect of our society, the sober portrait of its stratifications, their background and embattled contrasts. The facts sing for themselves."[43]

One-man exhibition, the Museum of Modern Art, New York, 1938: *American Photographs*, book reproducing 87 prints, with essay by Lincoln Kirstein, published by the Museum. Guggenheim Fellow, 1940.

Co-author with James Agee of *Let Us Now Praise Famous Men*, 1941. His portfolio of photographs and Agee's text "coequal, mutually independent, and fully collaborative." Agee explained that this extraordinary study of tenant families was intended to "be exhaustive, with no detail, however trivial it may seem, left untouched, no relevancy avoided, which lies within the power of remembrance to maintain, of the intelligence to perceive, and of the spirit to persist in."[44]

Now an associate editor of *Fortune* magazine.

Westchester County, N. Y., Farmhouse. 1931.   151

152   Penny Picture Display, Savannah. 1936.

Girl in Fulton Street, New York. 1929.   153

154   A Family Portrait. Alabama. 1936. From *Let Us Now Praise Famous Men* by James Agee and Walker Evans.

Garage in Southern City Outskirts. 1936.   155

156   Train East Will Be 40 Minutes Late (1955). Courtesy of *Fortune* Magazine.

The Grave of a Southern White. 1936.   157

158   Bed (1931).

Maine Pump. 1933. The Museum of Modern Art, New York.   159

HENRI CARTIER-BRESSON

Born in Chanteloup, France, 1908, of Norman mother, Parisian father. Had a passion for painting. Used Box Brownie at first only for amusing holiday snapshots; then began to learn how to make visual play with a camera. Excited by movies; "from some of the great. early films, I learned to look, and to see." At 20, decided against entering family business; studied painting two years with André Lhote; spent eight months in Cambridge, England, painting and attending literature courses. 1930, began to photograph seriously, at first influenced by Man Ray, then by Atget. 1931, to Africa; lived in native village on French Ivory Coast; photographed with a miniature camera but discovered when he developed his films on return to France that damp had gotten in. Had contracted blackwater fever; while recovering, traveled through Middle Europe and Italy. Discovered the Leica: "It became the extension of my eye and I have never been separated from it since I found it."[3] In Marseilles, "I prowled the streets all day, feeling very strung-up and ready to pounce, determined to 'trap' life—to preserve life in the act of living. Above all, I craved to seize the whole essence, in the confines of one single photograph, of some situation that was in the process of unrolling itself before my eyes."[3] 1933: to Italy and Spain; exhibition in Madrid. 1934: to Mexico with a film company that failed and left him close to stranded. Photographed; exhibited with Alvarez Bravo, Mexico City. 1935: to New York; exhibited with Walker Evans at Julien Levy Gallery.

1936: returned to France; worked with Jean Renoir as assistant on film, *Partie de Campagne*. 1937: married Ratna Mohini, Javanese dancer. Made documentary film of medical aid during Spanish Civil War, *Return to Life*. Began working for newspapers, magazines with Robert Capa, David Seymour ("Chim"), in the new medium of photo-reportage. "What does a 'picture story' mean? Life isn't made up of stories that you cut into slices like an apple pie. There's no standard way of approaching a story. We have to evoke a situation, a truth. This is the poetry of life's reality."[17]

Evolving his own approach, he sought to become as inconspicuous as possible: "Approach tenderly, gently . . . on tiptoe—even if the subject is still life. A velvet hand, a hawk's eye—these we should all have. . . . When the subject is in any way uneasy, the personality goes away where the camera can't find it. . . . It's as if you have thrown a stone in the water. You sometimes have to wait until all the waves are gone before the fishes come back again."[3] Of working with a 35mm. camera: "A contact sheet is so interesting because you see how a photographer thinks. He comes closer and closer to a subject, corrects it, looks at it again, and then, by very little movements, turns around it. . . . My contact sheets may be compared to the way you drive a nail into a plank. First you give several light

taps to build up a rhythm and align the nail with the wood. Then, much more quickly, and with as few strokes as possible, you hit the nail forcefully on the head and drive it in."[17]

1938: photographed Coronation in London, concentrating not on the crowns but on the crowds. Went on working with Jean Renoir on *La Règle du Jeu*. 1939, September: drafted into army. 1940: corporal in Film and Photo Unit; captured on Armistice Day. Three years as prisoner of war in Germany; escaped twice, was recaptured; succeeded the third time, in 1943, and joined his wife on a farm on the Loire. Got false papers; began working with underground, organizing photographic units which documented German occupation and retreat. 1945: made film for U. S. Office of War Information, *Le Retour*, showing return of prisoners of war to France.

1946: one man show at the Museum of Modern Art, New York; spent a year and a half in America, photographing throughout the country, sometimes on assignment. At that point, still regarded painting, photography, and the movies as "the gear shift of an automobile."[16]

In New York, in the spring of 1947, formed with Capa, Chim, George Rodger, William Vandivert, the photo agency Magnum, owned and directed by photographers to represent them while away: "What is most satisfying for a photographer is not recognition, success and so forth. It's communication; what you say can mean something to other people, can be of a certain significance. We have a great responsibility and must be extremely honest with what we see. . . . Magnum is important because there is somebody who represents our thinking when we may be thousands and thousands of miles away. For what is most important is that a picture which is a verb, an adjective, or a small link in the sentence, should remain a small link in the sentence and not be exaggerated. The tone, the intonation is important."[17] 1948: to the Far East for three years. In China, photographed Civil War; in India in 1949 Gandhi's funeral, for which he received Overseas Press Club Award. Then to Burma, Indonesia, Iran, Egypt—"Seeing in slices of one-hundredth second . . . spinning films out of myself like a silkworm."[1]

Returned to Europe, 1950. Published *The Decisive Moment (Image à la Sauvette)*, Paris and New York, 1952; *From One China to Another*, Paris, New York, London, 1954; *The Europeans*, Paris and New York, 1955; *Danses à Bali*, Paris, 1954. To Moscow, 1954; received another Overseas Press Club Award; published *People of Moscow*, New York, Paris, London, 1955. Large retrospective exhibition, initiated at Pavillon de Marsan, at the Louvre, Paris, 1957, traveling throughout Europe, Japan, the United States.

Madrid. Spain. 1933.   161

Andalusia, Spain. 1933.   163

164   Henri Matisse. 1944.

Abruzzi. 1953.   165

166   Cardinal Pacelli (later Pope Pius XII) at Montmartre, Paris. 1938.

The first flame of Gandhi's funeral pyre, Delhi. 1948.   167

168   Rice fields in Menangkabau country, Sumatra, Indonesia. 1950.

Moslem women praying, Kashmir. 1948.   169

170   Bargeman on Seine River. 1957.

Lourdes. 1958. 171

ANSEL ADAMS

Born San Francisco, 1902, of New England descent. During his childhood, the family fortune in timber and ships lost through succession of fires and shipwrecks; doubts raised by *The Education of Henry Adams*, a distant cousin, deepened depression. Disliked school; perplexed parents in 1915 bought him a year's pass to Golden Gate Fair; learned to use and demonstrate, to joy of exhibitors, various scientific and musical instruments. Had already taught himself piano; his playing attracted audiences.

At 14, visited Yosemite Valley; found its beauty and immensity "a culmination of experience so intense as to be almost painful. Since that day in 1916, my life has been colored and modulated by the great earth gesture of the Sierra."[45] Took first photographs there with Box Brownie. In San Francisco, studied processing with a photo-finisher who turned out a thousand prints a day. Returned every year to Yosemite and the High Sierra, exploring, photographing. Became ardent conservationist.

At 18, decided on music as profession. Was giving concerts and teaching piano when one evening in 1927 he met Albert Bender, unusual art patron; next morning Bender planned and raised funds for Adams' first portfolio of original photographs; instant acclaim. In 1928 married Virginia Best, also a musician and a mountaineer; two children born: Michael, 1933, Anne, 1936; home in Yosemite Valley.

In 1929, to New Mexico with Bender; met Mary Austin, John Marin, Georgia O'Keeffe, Paul Strand, whose negatives he found a revelation. *Taos Pueblo*, his first book of photographs, with text by Mary Austin, published 1930; enthusiastic response.

That year, stale from overpractice at piano, was advised to rest; Bender persuaded him to change profession to photography. Tackled new medium as if it were music; sought precise and flexible control, scientific reasons; read everything, asked questions, continually tested all materials and equipment: "Perfect technique is an attitude of mind. . . ." One morning awoke with a kind of vision of what photography could be: "It was like the Annunciation!" In 1931, with Edward Weston and Willard Van Dyke, founded Group f. 64.

In 1933 to New York; met Stieglitz, who looked at his prints and said, "Some of the most beautiful photographs I've ever seen in my life." One-man exhibition at *An American Place*, 1936.

First book on technique, *Making a Photograph*, 1935; first book of superb reproductions, *Sierra Nevada: the John Muir Trail*, 1937. Directed *Pageant of Photography* exhibition, San Francisco World's Fair, 1940, and that fall helped Beaumont Newhall found at the Museum of Modern Art, New York, the first department of photography as an art; served as vice-chairman of Advisory Board until 1946.

In 1941, was appointed photo-muralist to U. S. Department of the Interior; began photographing landscapes characteristic of various regions, as *Moonrise, Hernandez* for New Mexico. Project interrupted by World War II and never revived; Adams' interest continued. Early work had been intense, exquisite, often elegiac; now he began to master light, space, mood of huge landscapes. "Big country—space for heart and imagination. . . ."

During War, served as civilian consultant to armed services; pleaded cause of Japanese-Americans, incarcerated during hysteria after Pearl Harbor, in a book, *Born Free and Equal*, and an exhibition *Manzanar*, both 1944; poetic use of environment and affirmative approach.

In 1946, started first department teaching photography as a profession at the California School of Fine Arts. Received the same year, the first of two Guggenheim Fellowships which enabled him to photograph at their peaks of seasonal beauty the National Parks and Monuments throughout the United States, Alaska and Hawaii; photographed moods, "splendors and minutiae. . . . The grand landscapes and the blades of grass appear with equal eloquence."[46]

Between 1948 and 1950: began series of Basic Photo-Books, in which he presents his "philosophy of technique and application," which had crystallized as early as 1941 into the famous "Zone System," now widely recognized as basic approach to photography. Brought out *Portfolio One* and *Portfolio Two: The National Parks* of original prints in editions of 100 each. Published "bound portfolios" of magnificent reproductions, his own *My Camera in Yosemite Valley*, and *My Camera in the National Parks*, and Edward Weston's *My Camera on Point Lobos*. Illustrated John Muir's journals, *Yosemite and the Sierra Nevada*, and Mary Austin's *Land of Little Rain*.

In 1951, began collaboration with Nancy Newhall on regional articles, books: *Death Valley; Mission San Xavier del Bac*, and *A Pageant of History in Northern California*, all published 1954. Continued collaboration in exhibitions exploring potentials of words-and-photographs: *This is the American Earth*, on conservation, 1955; *I Hear America Singing* and *A Nation of Nations*, on America, with text by Walt Whitman, both for the United States Information Agency, 1957. With Edward Joesting, a book on Hawaii (in press 1958).

Serves as consultant on quality and performance of photographic materials to Polaroid Land Corporation. Teaches at Workshop in Yosemite every spring. Movie, *Ansel Adams, Photographer*, by David Myers, released 1957.

Feels much contemporary art "peripheral;" believes art must function; "I believe in growing things, and in things which have grown and died magnificently. I believe in people, and in the simple aspects of human life, and in the relation of man to nature. I believe man must be free, both in spirit and society, that he must build strength into himself, affirming 'the enormous beauty of the world' and acquiring the confidence to see and to express his vision. And I believe in photography as one means of expressing this affirmation, and of achieving an ultimate happiness and faith."[10]

ERECTED 1854.

Courthouse, Mariposa. 1934. George Eastman House, Rochester, N. Y.   173

174   White Tombstone, San Francisco. 1936.

Frozen Lake, Sierra Nevada. 1934. George Eastman House. Rochester. N. Y.   175

176   Alfred Stieglitz in An American Place. 1938. George Eastman House. Rochester. N. Y.

Mendocino County, California. 1950. 177

Moonrise, Hernandez, New Mexico. 1941.
George Eastman House, Rochester, N. Y.   179

180   Edward Weston. 1950. George Eastman House. Rochester, N. Y.

Mono Lake. California. 1944. George Eastman House. Rochester. N. Y. 181

Sierra Nevada from Lone Pine. California. 1944. George Eastman House. Rochester. N. Y.   183

184   Refugio Beach, California. 1947. George Eastman House. Rochester. N. Y.

Aspens, Autumn. 1944. George Eastman House, Rochester, N. Y.   185

Mt. Williamson—Clearing Storm. 1944.

George Eastman House, Rochester, N. Y.

A NOTE ON TECHNIQUES

From 1839 to 1851 there were two rival processes: the daguerreotype and the calotype. These gave way in the late 1850s to collodion negatives which were printed on albumen paper, gold-toned. Around 1880 gelatino-bromide emulsion, invented in 1871 by Richard Leach Maddox, an English physician, was perfected and has been used ever since for making negatives, either on glass plates or film. A variety of printing processes were popular between 1890 and 1920, when most photographers standardized on collodio-bromide papers for contact printing or enlarging.

Except where otherwise noted, the originals reproduced in this book are either gold-toned albumen prints from collodion negatives or collodio-bromide prints from dry plates or film.

CALOTYPE. A paper negative process invented by William Henry Fox Talbot in England in 1840; became obsolete in 1851.

COLLODION PROCESS, COLLODION NEGATIVE. The first practical method of making glass negatives, invented in England in 1851 by Frederick Scott Archer. Glass plates were flowed with collodion in which a soluble halide had been dissolved. While the surface was still tacky, the plate was plunged into silver-nitrate solution, thus forming light-sensitive silver halides. The plates had to be made, exposed, and developed all within 15 minutes, while still wet; consequently the photographer working in the field had to carry a darkroom with him wherever he went. Became obsolete about 1880, when gelatin dry plates were perfected.

DAGUERREOTYPE. A direct positive process invented by Jacques Louis Mandé Daguerre and published by the French Government in 1839. Silvered copper plates were polished mirror bright, then made light-sensitive by fuming them with iodine. After exposure, the latent image was developed by exposure to the fumes of heated mercury, which formed, in proportion to the light received, an amalgam as delicate as the dust on a butterfly's wing. With the invention of the collodion process, it became obsolescent, and was hardly ever practiced after 1860.

GUM PRINT. *See* Pigment Print.

PALLADIUM PRINT, PALLADIOTYPE. Paper made light-sensitive with the salts of palladium. Used as a substitute for platinum paper, which it resembles, during World War 1 and for some years thereafter. Became obsolete about 1930.

PHOTOGRAVURE. A graphic arts process for the reproduction of photographs with printer's ink. An intaglio copper plate is made from the original photograph, which is then printed like an engraving. The process is currently used in fine book production; its use to produce small editions of single prints is infrequent.

PIGMENT PRINT. Paper made light-sensitive by coating it with a mixture of a colloid, a pigment, and potassium bichromate. On exposure to light, the colloid is hardened and rendered insoluble. "Development" consists simply in washing away with water the unexposed areas. When the colloid is gum arabic, the process is known as "gum printing." Pigment printing allows the photographer great control, for he can wash away any part of the image with hot water, can resensitize the print and give it a second exposure beneath the negative. Popular from about 1895 to 1915.

PLATINUM PRINT, PLATINOTYPE. Paper made light-sensitive with the salts of platinum. Characteristics: great permanence, long tonal scale, delicacy of greys, and tendency to give soft results. Invented by William Willis in England in 1873; commercial production of platinum paper discontinued about 1930.

PLATINUM AND FERROPRUSSIATE PRINT. A platinum print resensitized with iron salt solution which, on a second exposure and "development" with water, gives a blue-green or blue tone.

STEREOGRAPH. Word coined by Oliver Wendell Holmes to describe the double photograph which when viewed through a stereoscope gives the illusion of three dimensions.

SELECTED BIBLIOGRAPHY

GENERAL

Freund, Gisèle. *La Photographie en France au dix-neuvième siècle.* Paris: La Maison des Amis des Livres. 1936.

Gernsheim, Helmut & Gernsheim, Alison. *The History of Photography.* London: Oxford University Press, 1955.

Newhall, Beaumont. *The History of Photography.* New York: The Museum of Modern Art, 1948.

Newhall, Beaumont, ed. *On Photography.* Watkins Glen, N. Y.: Century House, 1956.

Taft, Robert. *Photography and the American Scene.* New York: The Macmillan Company, 1938.

MONOGRAPHS

ATGET. *Atget, photographe de Paris.* Préface par Pierre MacOrlan. New York: E. Weyhe, about 1930.

CAMERON. *Victorian Photographs of Famous Men & Fair Women.* With introductions by Virginia Woolf and Roger Fry. London: The Hogarth Press, 1926.—Gernsheim, Helmut. *Julia Margaret Cameron.* London: The Fountain Press, 1948.

CARTIER-BRESSON. Kirstein, Lincoln & Newhall, Beaumont. *The Photographs of Henri Cartier-Bresson.* New York: The Museum of Modern Art, 1947.

EMERSON. Newhall, Nancy. "Emerson's Bombshell," *Photography,* I (Winter. 1947). 50–52. 110ff.

GARDNER. Cobb. Josephine. "Alexander Gardner." *Image,* VII (June, 1958). 124–36.

HILL. Schwarz. Heinrich. *David Octavius Hill, Master of Photography.* New York: The Viking Press. 1931.

LANGE. Dixon. Daniel. "Dorothea Lange." *Modern Photography,* XVI (Dec.. 1952). 68–77. 138–41.

O'SULLIVAN. Baumhofer. Hermine M.. "T. H. O'Sullivan." *Image,* II (April. 1953). 20–21.

SALOMON. Hunter. Peter. "Salomon." *Photography,* XII (Jan 1957), 32–37. 47.—Safranski. Kurt. "Dr. Salomon." *Popular Photography,* XXIII (August, 1948). 56–59. 104ff.

SOUTHWORTH & HAWES. Newhall. Beaumont. "First American Masters of the Camera." *Art News Annual 1948,* p. 91–98. 168–72.

STEICHEN. Sandburg. Carl. *Steichen the Photographer.* New York: Harcourt. Brace and Company. 1929.

STIEGLITZ. Frank, Waldo; Norman, Dorothy; & others, eds. *America & Alfred Stieglitz: A Collective Portrait.* Garden City, N. Y.: Doubleday, Doran & Company, Inc., 1934.

STRAND. Newhall. Nancy. *Paul Strand Photographs, 1915–1945.* New York: The Museum of Modern Art. 1945.

WESTON. Newhall, Nancy. *The Photographs of Edward Weston.* New York: The Museum of Modern Art, 1946.

SOURCES OF QUOTATIONS

1. Conversation or unpublished letter.

2. Weston, Edward. "Photography—Not Pictorial." *Camera Craft*, XXXVII (1930), 313–20. (Reprinted in Newhall. *On Photography*.)

3. Cartier-Bresson. Henri. *The Decisive Moment*. New York: Simon and Schuster, 1952. (Introduction reprinted in part in Newhall, *On Photography*.)

4. Weston, Edward. Unpublished *Day Books*.

5. Cameron, Julia Margaret. "The Annals of My Glass House." *Photographic Journal*, LXVII (July, 1927), 296–301. Also published in Gernsheim, Helmut, *Julia Margaret Cameron*, pp. 67–72.

6. Strand, Paul, "The Art Motive in Photography," *British Journal of Photography*, LXX (1923), 613–614. (Excerpts reprinted in Newhall, *On Photography*.)

7. Weston, Edward. *My Camera on Point Lobos*. Yosemite National Park: Virginia Adams; Boston: Houghton Mifflin Company, 1950.

8. Stieglitz, Alfred, "Why I Photograph Clouds," *Amateur Photographer* LVI (Sept. 19, 1923), 255.

9. Bry, Doris, "Alfred Stieglitz Photographer." Introduction to catalogue of Stieglitz Exhibition, National Gallery of Art, Washington, D.C., Mar. 15 to Apr. 27, 1958.

10. Adams, Ansel, "Personal Credo," *American Annual of Photography for 1944*, pp. 7–16. (Reprinted in Newhall, *On Photography*.)

11. Newhall, Nancy, ed., "Edward Weston: Photographer," *Aperture*, VI, No. 1 (1958), 1–50.

12. Reilly, Rose, "Steichen—the Living Legend," *Popular Photography*, II (March, 1938), 10–12, 88–91.

13. Stieglitz, Alfred, "The Magazine 291 and The Steerage," *Twice-A-Year*, Double No. VIII–IX (1942), 131–36.

14. Cobb, Darius, "Mental and Moral Training in Photography," *Photo Era*, III (1900), 361–65.

15. Taft, Robert. *Photography and the American Scene*. New York: The Macmillan Company, 1938.

16. Kirstein, Lincoln and Newhall, Beaumont. *The Photographs of Henri Cartier-Bresson*. New York: The Museum of Modern Art, 1947.

17. Dobell, Byron, "A Conversation with Henri Cartier-Bresson," *Popular Photography*, XLI (September, 1957), 130–32.

18. Adams, Ansel. Introduction to his *Portfolio One: Twelve Photographic Prints*. San Francisco, 1948.

19. Stieglitz, Alfred. Introduction to catalogue of exhibition of his photographs at the Anderson Galleries, New York, 1921. (Reprinted in Newhall. *On Photography*.)

20. Stokes, I. N. Phelp. *The Hawes-Stokes Collection of American Daguerreotypes by Albert Sands Southworth and Josiah Johnson Hawes*. New York: The Metropolitan Museum of Art. 1939.

21. Hawes, Josiah Johnson. "Stray Leaves from the Diary of the Oldest Professional Photographer in the World." *Photo Era*, XVI (Feb. 1906), 104–107.

22. Newhall, Beaumont. "First American Masters of the Camera." *Art News Annual 1948*, pp. 91–98, 168–72.

23. Southworth, Albert S., "An Address to the National Photographic Association of the United States. Delivered at Cleveland . . . 1870." *Philadelphia Photographer*, VIII (1871), 315–23.

24. Specification for U. S. Patent 12,700, dated April 10, 1855.

25. Cobb, Josephine, "Alexander Gardner," *Image*, VII (June, 1958), 124–36.

26. Wheeler, G. M. *Preliminary Report . . . Explorations and Surveys Principally in Nevada and Arizona*. Washington: 1872

27. Cameron, Julia Margaret. *Victorian Photographs of Famous Men & Fair Women*. With introductions by Virginia Woolf and Roger Fry. London: The Hogarth Press, 1926.

28. Obituary of Julia Margaret Cameron. reprinted from *The World* in *British Journal of Photography*, XXVI (Mar. 7, 1879), 116.

29. Gernsheim, Helmut. *Julia Margaret Cameron*. London: The Fountain Press, 1948.

30. Emerson, P. H., "An Ideal Photographic Exhibition," *The Amateur Photographer*, II (Oct. 23, 1885), 431.

31. Emerson, P. H. *Pictures of East Anglian Life*. London: Sampson Low, Marston, Searle & Rivington, 1888.

32. Emerson, P. H., "Photography a Pictorial Art," *The Amateur Photographer*, III (Mar. 19, 1886), 138–39.

33. Sandburg, Carl. *Steichen the Photographer*. New York: Harcourt, Brace and Company, 1929.

34. *Infinity*, published by American Society of Magazine Photographers, Dec. 1954-Jan. 1955. Special Steichen issue, containing conversation between Steichen and Wayne Miller recorded on film for TV presentation by N.B.C., Jan. 30, 1955. Copyright by NBC. Quoted by permission.

35. Calmettes, André. Letter to Berenice Abbott. Unpublished.

36. Strand, Paul, "Photography to Me," *Minicam Photography*, VIII (May, 1945), 42–46, 86, 90.

37. Stieglitz. Alfred, "Our Illustrations," *Camera Work*, No. 49–50 (June, 1917), 36.

38. Strand, Paul and Roy, Claude. *La France de profil*. Lausanne: La Guilde du Livre, 1952.

39. Safranski, Kurt, "Dr. Salomon," *Popular Photography*, XXIII (August, 1948), 56–59, 104ff.

40. Salomon, Erich. *Berühmte Zeitgenossen in unbewachten Augenblicken*. Stuttgart, J. Engelhorns Nachf., 1931.

41. Dixon, Daniel, "Dorothea Lange," *Modern Photography*, XVI (Dec., 1952), 68–77, 138–41.

42. Lorentz, Pare, "Dorothea Lange, Camera with a Purpose," *U. S. Camera 1941*, I. 93–98.

43. Evans, Walker. *American Photographs*. New York: Museum of Modern Art, 1938.

44. Agee, James and Evans, Walker. *Let Us Now Praise Famous Men*. Boston: Houghton Mifflin Company, 1941.

45. Muir, John and Adams, Ansel. *Yosemite and the Sierra Nevada*. Boston: Houghton Mifflin Company, 1948.

46. Adams, Ansel. *My Camera in the National Parks*. Yosemite National Park: Virginia Adams; Boston: Houghton Mifflin Company, 1950.

INDEX

Titles and references to titles of photographs are in italics.

The composition for this book was done by Westcott & Thomson, Inc., the engravings by Gatchel & Manning Co.; the design and layout by the authors and T. E. Mergendahl, Jr.